This Side of Yesterday:
Extinction or Utopia

*By natural laws the earth stays on a course;
increasingly its operation and its destiny are
determined by the hands and minds of man. Never
has man's omnipotence been so great, and never
have his shortcomings been so evident.*

*Despite unmatched affluence the human species is
moving into a dark and degradative period. The questions
are why, and can there be a different course.*

This Side of Yesterday: Extinction or Utopia

Paul S. Henshaw
University of Arizona

John Wiley & Sons, Inc.
New York · London · Sydney · Toronto

233892

Preface

This is a book about man in the process of becoming. It grew out of experience in preparing for and teaching broad-scope courses such as "Science and Society," "Population Behavior," and "The Evolution of Man" in a university setting. It draws also from a broader background of experimental biology, environmental radiation, systems science, and human behavior as seen especially in brain-injured children.

In the process of tracing man's ancestry, his origin, and the determinants of his character—the features that have caused man to be set apart—one is brought face to face with man's heredity, his motivational drives, his assumed prerogatives, and his ethical codes, all of which combine to make man the behaving and reacting organism that he is. By consideration of the different elements in relation to the earth as a closed ecosystem and to the uncompromising laws of Nature, one is confronted with tendencies and conduct that are inconsistent, contradictory, and irreconcilable—indeed, with strong degradative processes that are working their devious influence despite evidence on every hand of peak affluence generally throughout the world.

The first part of this book—Chapters 3 to 5, in particular—deals with the making of man and with his tendencies and behavior as they have come to be. This has been done by utilizing newer knowledge derived from systems analysis, cybernetic function, information biology, and ecosystems operation. Chapters 6 to 8 discuss man's societal behavior and give a profound castigation of his use of his most precious asset—his intellect. Chapters 9 to 12, then, deal with the inevitability of major changes in man as a behaving societal creature, taking into account the practices and trends, as established, and the adjustments and adaptations required for a strong human role in Nature's ongoing scheme.

The evolution-of-man approach enables and requires multiple factor analysis with evaluation and recognition of the relative strength of component determiners. It is by means of an integrated picture that impressions are gained of full operational behavior and of the price to be paid for maintenance of the human preferential position. Inherent is the philosophy of comparative risks and awareness of the momentous decisions that cannot be avoided.

The term "Nature," as explained at the end of the book, has been used in a special way. The meaning intended in all cases is the *system of all phenomena in space and time*, but I have personalized the phenomena, endowing them imaginatively with personality and individuality. This has been for convenience in dealing with the issue between natural forces on the one hand and the mind-of-man on the other.

I express indebtedness to Newell Younggren, Chairman of the Department of Biological Sciences at the University of Arizona, for assistance, without which this development would have been much more difficult. Also I express appreciation to Walter Claus, former Assistant Director, Division of Biology and Medicine, U.S. Atomic Energy Commission; to Sylvan Kaplan, Chief, Division of Plans and Objectives, National Park Service, U.S. Department of Interior; to Walter Munster, Chief, Policy Branch, Division of International Affairs. U.S. Atomic Energy Commission; to Millicent Pommerenke, authoress; to George Sakalosky, Staff assistant to the Chairman, U.S. Atomic Energy Commission; and to John Staley, now Professor of Sociology, Brigham Young University, whose philosophical thoughts and wise counsel have contributed to various of the ideas expressed here.

PAUL S. HENSHAW

Contents

This Side of Yesterday:
Extinction or Utopia

Chapter 1

Collision Course

At the same time, mankind stands at the pinnacle of success and is threatened with catastrophic degradation.

Strong natural forces are impelling a choice between extinction and survival—in reality, a choice between extinction and utopia, inasmuch as survival in the future will require a saner and therefore more secure and more rewarding form of life. A choice is inevitable. It will be by default if not by design.

It is apparent to thoughtful people everywhere that human society is on a collision course. Freedom to procreate with abandon, to pollute without restraint, and to exploit with increasing intensity, quite obviously cannot go on indefinitely. Clearly something has got to give—and soon. It is fully evident that in the process of change, species man will either drop into oblivion or ascend to magnificent new heights of civilization simply by meeting the requirements for remaining existent.

In dealing with the question of extinction or survival, there is no middle ground. By meeting minimum requirements for survival, the conditions for achieving a utopian situation will automatically be met at the same time. With requirements and demands being what they are for survival, either the human species will make peace with Nature, or Nature will sweep the human species aside—and with great finality.

With his intellect and his inventiveness, man has created inundative and overkill potential of vast proportions. To avoid the obliterative consequences will require a way of life with moral and ethical standards well beyond those of the present period. Problems of the present period extend beyond availability of money or technical know-how; they involve purpose and goals. They involve commitments by factions of people and by the species as a whole as to whether we as a people are concerned only with life for the moment or look forward to long-range survival as a species. Increasingly, the human species is being impelled to reexamine its instinctive drives, its traditional motivations, and its aspirations to see if they are compatible with prospects for continuing species life. People generally are being forced, despite powerful inertia, to ask again what it is that makes life worthwhile—what it is that causes a human being toward the end of his life to say: "I am glad I have lived." Moreover, the human species is being impelled to do these things taking into account what Nature will tolerate—Nature being the actual and the real.

This book is about man—man as he is today—the way he got to be as he is, the compulsions and drives that rule him, and the steps he is being compelled to take if species survival is to endure. Since opting for a new way of life is the only selection that makes sense, when the choice is between extinction and survival, the fixation here will be on the transformation that we assume must take place very soon or that is already in the making.

In dealing with man, the creature of intellect, and planet earth as a limited entity, the effort will be to bring the facts of science and the elements of common sense and clear reasoning to bear as much as possible. Automatically, this will bring us face to face with confrontations and thoughts about a utopian situation—indeed the prospect and the necessity of accepting and fostering now a far more perfect world society than most people have regarded as possible. One of the questions, assuming that a utopian situation could somehow be achieved, will be that of whether a utopian type of life would be tolerable—indeed, whether a stable kind of life can be made to go hand-in-hand with the kinds of activity that will prove "rewarding" and "satisfying."

The task at first is to comprehend the creature called "man," how he came to have unusual powers of intellect, and how, at the same time, these powers have placed his species in a position of uniqueness, ascendency, and great vulnerability. Next, steps are taken to identify and characterize the underlying drives and the ethical motivations that make the human species behave as it does. Finally, the position will be that further expansion and application of the evolving mental potential will be the only means of escape from the growing dilemma. The author is thus pessimistic but hopeful. When the factual evidence is in, he becomes militant in insisting that no ground be left unturned in preparation for a new way of life.

There are also things this book is not. First, it is not revolutionary. The view is that civilization, despite obvious errors and inefficiencies, has provided much that is good and could not readily be replaced if destroyed. Second, it is not antiprogress as some writings are at this time. It recognizes the necessity of continuing development and advancement if the human species is to remain a part of Nature's scheme and if the human mind is to fulfill itself as the central feature of human existence. Third, it is not a propagandistic or political action document. It does not implore people to take action for the public good. Instead, it points out the hard facts of Nature and then calls attention to steps that must be taken as a minimum if human beings are even to have a place in the natural order. Fourth, it is not a treatise of nuclear weapons, nerve gases, or psychological warfare as the main basis for fear of extinction, although some reference will be made to these elements. Emphasis instead is on the question of sustaining power of the earth under increasing demands.

Furthermore, this book is not about the welfare of nations, as such, the view being that nationalism and international power politics are pretty much panoply of the past. Force and multiples of overkill as means of fixing relationships between factions of people, becomes increasingly ludicrous. The search is for values and goals compatible with man's position and posture at this, our own stage, in Nature's ongoing scheme.

NATURE'S INEXORABLE PROGRESSION

At short range—let us say, in terms of actual human experience —the earth appears to change very little. The seasons are observed to come and go and organisms to live and die, but the general design and operation of the earth gives the impression of remaining much the same. At long range the picture is quite different.

From studies in geology, astronomy, chemistry, biology, and

other sciences, it is clear that change has been a dominant feature of Nature. It is evident not only that the earth had a beginning and evolved to its present stage, but also that this sequence is but one of multitudinous types of change occurring continuously in the vast universe around us. Impressions are that because of interactions of certain elements of the universe, about 5 to 6 billion years ago, the earth was formed from gaseous materials split off from a vast interstellar cloud as it was giving rise to the sun and its planets (Gerard Kuiper, Chapter 2, *The Earth and Its Atmosphere*, edited by D.R. Bates, 1957). Indications are that over long periods of time the gases condensed and formed molecules, simpler ones at first and then increasingly complex ones, leading thereby to formation of substances that came eventually to comprise the land, the oceans and the atmosphere. It is clear that volcanos occurred and that mountains pushed up only to be torn down and rebuilt again—in geologic time. Late in this sequence, life appeared, and still later, species man came into being—all as part of an on-going and seemingly unending pattern. Here it is important to be aware that other concepts of the earth's origin are available in addition to the one set forth by Kuiper. All, however, involve the idea of gaseous elements and simpler inorganic compounds at the beginning.

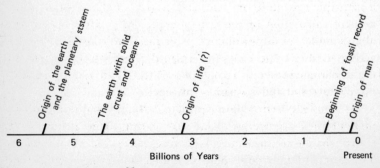

Fig. 1. Time sequence of key events.

Figure 1 pictures a sequential relationship of key events in a history involving planet earth. It contains implications of particular importance to the thesis being developed: (1) that the earth and universe are dynamic rather than static—that is, changing, (2) that a vast process is in motion and progressing, although the destination is by no means apparent, (3) that man is a very late product of this ongoing operation, and (4) that there is great flexibility in Nature's functional pattern.

RIGIDITY

Equally impressive are Nature's uncompromising laws. Although there is great flexibility in Nature's operational pattern and in the pathways followed, there is extreme rigidity of natural laws by means of which action is taken to achieve the different operative functions. Consider the compound interest law. As long as there is compounding, growth occurs and ever faster. This is the way money on interest increases in amount and earning power. It is the way populations grow and cultures of organisms multiply. There is also the mass action law, which operates in the opposite direction, characterizing diminishment and deterioration, as in the case of radioactive decay of elements. There is the law of supply and demand. As commodities become scarce, the demand becomes greater, and when the supply is exhausted there is no more irrespective of the demand.

There is Ohm's law which indicates that electrical current is equal to potential or voltage divided by the resistance of the circuit—that is, when the units in each case are defined concretely and in a certain way. Consider also the laws of statistics. Probability is a fact of Nature. It is unchanging and unchangeable as a principle or condition. The same is true of the constant Pi as used in calculation of the circumference of a circle. There are almost endless examples of laws, principles, and constants that are acting to direct the course of natural processes. Important to the development here is recognition of the rigidity and unchanging character of the governing influences.

To ignore Nature's laws, principles, and conditions, or to pretend they do not exist and go against them, is futile—in reality disastrous inasmuch as nature makes no compromises. The latter, we may point out, is another unvarying natural law. The things of Nature, including living things and man, are

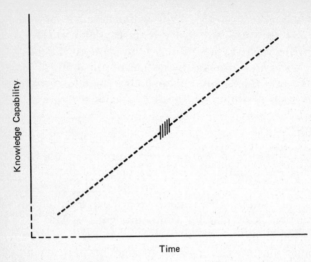

Fig. 2. Man's knowability.

governed by natural laws, and to presume or to act otherwise is unrealistic.

LIMITS OF KNOWLEDGE

In commenting broadly about Nature, as we are doing, it is important to consider the limits of knowledge and the confidence we can have in ideas of any sort offered as factual. Figure 2 is a representation of the situation as visualized. Notice the coordinates. The abscissas show time and the ordinates represent knowledge. Inferences are that with time, knowledge increases. Since there is no way of knowing when time began nor when knowledge as such first existed, it is necessary to show the beginning parts of the coordinates as dotted. Similarly, since there is so much information about the past that would be knowable but that is unavailable, and since there is so much information about the future that at the present stage would be impossible even to comprehend, it is necessary to show the curve of knowledge as dotted except for a very small segment in the middle relating to the present period. The view is that only a very small portion of the information that is knowable is available to us as human beings at the present time, despite our great intellect and the information explosion of the past few decades.

Although it is necessary to recognize straightforwardly that only a small portion of that which is knowable is known, it is essential to recognize at the same time that at our period in time there is available a substantial—actually vast—body of well-verified and tested information. Also there is a substantial amount of well-reasoned conjecture to serve as guiding thoughts.

Knowledge in itself is a phenomenology. It constitutes a power and an influence, depending on its integrity, reliability, and significance. Actually, knowledge constitutes greater power in the present period than it has in the past simply because it is more advanced. As will be revealed in this book, man's position of increasing control over the affairs of planet earth has come primarily from his ability to generate, process, and use information.

Here, we shall utilize rational conjecture as well as facts, making evident as much as possible where one leaves off and the other begins. The reader probably will be impressed with how far present knowledge can and does carry in comprehending the nature of man and his problems. Moreover, it is to be expected that broad new vistas of understanding will continue to open up to us in the future, as long as the spirit of inquiry continues in the minds of men.

Whether there is an end to knowledge—a point at which all that is knowable becomes known—is in itself an arresting question. A view set forth and supported here is that *information interacting with information is generative,* thus causing the knowable to expand. This too, it appears, is one of Nature's fundamental laws, and one most important in our own time.

THE EARTH AND MAN AS FEATURES

In the exploration and analysis of Nature's operation, we start with an accepted bias. It is that somehow the earth and man are special. The earth is where life and intellect began and it is where the human species came into being. It is therefore *us* and our home that we are talking about, and perhaps a certain amount of self-interest can be regarded not only as justifiable, but also as a primary element in the overall scheme of things.

We shall look objectively at Nature's operation, constantly keeping human welfare and human benefits in mind.

Actually when one examines the vantage point from which human beings observe Nature's operations, the earth and man indeed are special. They are special because of their uniqueness. It is possible, of course, that life and intellect, or elements similar, may have arisen elsewhere in the universe, but even if that is so, it is only the life and intellect on planet earth that we are privileged to know about thus far. Obviously we can deal only with that which is available to us to observe and analyze. As has been the situation continuously, deductions must be altered as more reliable information is developed.

Later, we consider the requirements for long-range survival of the human species—the steps that of necessity must be taken to cause Nature, in accordance with her rigid laws, to tolerate, to sustain, and to permit human progress for a long time in the future. The question will not be so much, "Will this occur?" but, "What will be required to make it occur?"

The problems of what rights and prerogatives are justifiable for the human species within the confines of planet earth and Nature's laws, and whether the human species should struggle for a preferential position, are points to be considered. The view to be presented is that the human species must endure and has an obligation to itself to endure—with great tenaciousness, using means that not only are in accordance with Nature's unrelenting laws but that agree with selected moral standards of right and wrong. The position will be that the human species should transform, advancing to new levels of specialization and accomplishment, doing so at a rate commensurate with opportunities and Nature's limiting requirements.

THE EARTH AS A CLOSED ECOSYSTEM

Central to our thesis is the idea that planet earth is essentially a limited entity—one that receives little from the outside and gives off little. As a limited or closed entity, the earth is like a culture tube of broth into which bacteria can be introduced and observed to multiply and grow. The earth in fact is a kind of "culture tube." In time it came to have certain nutrient materials, and through spontaneous generation and evolution has inoculated itself with a large number of organisms of many types, including human beings.

In case of the bacterial culture tube, we know what happens following inoculation. When the broth is rich and nutritious, growth is rapid. At intervals of a few minutes or an hour or more, depending especially on temperature, each bacterium divides, causing the number to double. At this stage, growth is in accord with the compound interest law mentioned earlier—that is, becoming faster and faster. As time passes, however, the elements of nutrition thin out, and waste products accumulate, causing the growth to slow and eventually to come to a standstill. The process is characterized by the familiar S-shaped growth curve (Figure 3). The action is strictly in accord with Nature's general law of supply and demand, mentioned earlier. When food is abundant, growth is rapid, and when food is scarce, growth slows and eventually comes to a standstill—at which stage the organisms die unless the food supply is somehow replenished.

Since the earth is a kind of culture tube inoculated with people (and other organisms), the same general laws and prin-

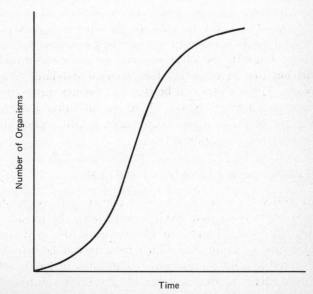

Fig. 3. S-shaped growth curve.

ciples apply. When the resources were vast and the number of people small, comparatively, the population increase occurred in accordance with the early phase of the growth curve, Figure 3. As we change from the Era of Expansion (when new territories were yet to be discovered and developed) to the Era of Concentration (when the growth increment of people each year must be accommodated entirely in the same territory instead of by migration of at least some to new lands), Nature's harsh law of supply and demand begins to impose its restraints. Without adequate conservation measures, as we know so well, such restraints may become so severe that it causes widespread deterioration and even the death of whole populations.

In addition to the culture tube as a model support system, consider also the *balanced aquarium*—the beautiful desk-sized tank maintained by fanciers in such a way that there is an interchange of materials between plants and animals so delicately balanced that no supply of food from the outside is necessary, nor is there a significant accumulation of waste. In such systems there is a recycling of elements. Oxygen given off by the plants is used by the animals, and carbon dioxide given off by the animals is used by the plants, and so on. Such a model is important when consideration is given to the earth as a closed ecosystem. Inherent are two noteworthy features. One is the idea that the species maintained are carefully selected by the designer, and the other is that the designer himself sets the balance. There is preferential treatment of species and there is management of high order.

As implied above, the earth is not a completely closed system. Although this fact will not alter the generalizations being made about the earth as a limited entity, it is important that we take cognizance of the actual situation. Energy from the sun in vast quantities comes to the earth each day. As commonly known, the sun's energy is employed by Nature in the process of photosynthesis and thereby in the production of plant forms. When evaluating carefully the sustaining power of the earth, this feature must be considered.

MEETING MINIMUM REQUIREMENTS

Acceptance of the earth as a closed ecosystem is but one central concept that of necessity must be considered in planning for the period just ahead. Another—one very different but equally important, or more so—is the idea that species man has certain special requirements simply because man is a creature of intellect. From studies in a number of fields, such as general education, child psychology, and mental health, we are painfully aware of the stultification and suffocation that results from a lack of challenge—that is, from a lack of opportunity to nourish curiosity and inventiveness. Two strong forces are acting to suppress the emergence, the quality, or the spirit that is human. One is the oppression coming from growing complexity caused by increasing numbers of people and expanding technology, and the other is the tightening influence of custom, tradition, and institutionalization.

One of the strongest points of this book will be the view that human beings, if they are to remain human, must have unfettered opportunity for growth of intellect—indeed for expression of the human spirit. In the Era of Concentration, the task is to foresee and to plan for the future as effectively as our pioneer forefathers foresaw and planned for the Era of Expansion.

Founders of the government of the United States took into account certain unalienable rights and the importance of individual expression. It cost them a revolution to launch their ideas, but their product has stood the test of nearly 200 years—a very long time in the history of governments and in the history of ways of living. In our era, we are called on to do as well in assessing needs and in meeting requirements. We offer the thought that with the intellectual resources at our command, we cannot be judged as doing nearly as well unless we do far better.

IMPOSED CHOICE

No complicated mathematics is required to reveal that with continued expansion of human needs, a break in the earth's sustaining power will occur in the foreseeable future. Consider the following. When the population increase (margin of births over deaths) is one percent per year, the time required to double the population is approximately 70 years and when two percent, it is slightly more than 35 years. These are mathematical facts. The increase rate in the United States at the present time is a little over one percent, and for the world it is close to two percent. By using the last figure, it is easy to show by calculation that with continuing growth rates of the present, a period of only about 600 years will be required to have one person for each square foot of land area on the face of the earth, literally standing room only. This is a short period in human history, and it is obvious that unless man takes deliberate steps in advance to reduce his growth rate, Nature, by means of pollution, congestion, and violence, will force a reduction long before the standing-room situation is reached.

Actually, as we know all too well already, generalized degradation in the form of pollution, congestion, deteriorating power sources, and violence is occurring now and is expanding rapidly. Increasingly, people are arming in their homes and automobiles, and more and more our young people are feeling frustration about what the future can hold for them. The thesis put forth here is that a *stultification crisis* has come upon the human species during the present generation, and that near superhuman effort will be required to avoid an accelerating deterioration.

A still stronger thesis from the outset is that survival of the human species in the period ahead will not depend so much on people opting for what they want by the democratic process, but instead on coming to terms with Nature in a realistic way. Facing the problems realistically will be harsh and brutal inasmuch as cherished values, customs, and institutions emergent and valuable during the pioneer period will of necessity be questioned and in many instances revised or discarded.

A head-in-the-sand approach in dealing with cultural problems in the Era of Concentration, obviously, will be fatal. Irrespective of a reluctance on the part of people generally to alter a way of life, or of power structures to countenance change, we assume that usually when people are forced to make a choice between extinction and survival, even though survival will require goals that effectively utopian and thus essentially impossible to attain, they will opt for survival regardless of sacrifice.

Ours is a moment of decision; it is a time when a choice is being made by default if not by design. It is a moment when a test of man's will is being made—a determination of whether man as a species has the stamina and fortitude to choose and act for adjustment and continuing advancement instead of being content with life as usual and with growing degradation and eventual oblivion.

Chapter 2

Man's Place in Nature's Scheme

Cosmology is a term used to connote change in the universe. It implies that evolution is occurring in and among the stars and planets the same as it is on planet earth and that there is a progression in the overall process. As already discussed, formation of the earth was an event in the history of the universe and the emergence of man was an event in the history of the earth. Both are events in the general cosmology.

Man as a physical entity is composed of elements of the earth. Man as we know him came from the earth. If hominoid creatures—creatures with some form of intellect—exist on other stars or planets, we assume that they arose from the elements of those other bodies and not from the elements of earth.

There are four pertinent facts to be recognized in our quest for better understanding the nature of man and why the human species is in such a manifold predicament at the present time.

1. The existence of man is part of a general process—an event in a very long series of events that have gone before. Without any doubt, man is part of a system that is leading somewhere. Man is part of something that is in motion—dynamic. Man is part of a grand cavalcade of change occurring in the universe. The goal of Nature's grand cavalcade is not apparent, but it is clear that man is part of the system and contributes to the progression.

2. Equally important, man's existence and behavior are governed by the same uncompromising laws that are applied by Nature in dealing with other elements of the universe. Man, being comprised of the elements of Nature, is subject to the

Laws of Nature. In this respect man is not different from other entities in Nature's grand system.

3. Also fundamental is the fact that despite the rigidity of laws applied by Nature in governing her processes, the direction of her action appears to be random. Said in another way, the course followed by Nature in her progression is the path of least resistance. The meaning, nevertheless, is the same. The direction is uncharted, the objectives are unspecified. Most important, the direction is subject to modification by a guiding influence.

4. The culminating point then is that inasmuch as Nature's direction is uncharted and can be augmented, it is subject to willful manipulation by an intelligence such as that possessed by human beings.

These four facts place the human species in an inspiring and genuinely omnipotent position in the overall cosmology, all of which makes the main questions more intriguing. How did man, the creature with advanced intellect, come into being? Why has Nature produced only one surviving species of this type? How has the human species, with its uniqueness and its vast potential, become a major threat to itself? Have other species behaved in such a way as to threaten their own survival? Further insight comes from consideration of still other principles.

ORGANIZATION AND DISORGANIZATION

Inherent in Nature's operations are the processes of building up and tearing down. Mountains are formed only to be eroded away and built again. Trees rise only to wither, die, disintegrate and again form. Human beings grow, mature, become old, expire, and live again through their offspring. So very often the processes of organization and disorganization are observed together. In combination, they are seen as fundamental in the processes of life and intellect, and in the operation of Nature in general.

For the purposes here, life is defined as a kind of sustained interaction among the elements of nature—one in which the forces for organization are greater than the forces for disorganization, leaving a margin for life and thereby the attributes of behavior. Most vital organs of the body have a margin of reserve.

Consider, for example, the blood-forming organs, meaning especially the bone marrow, lymph nodes, and spleen. Normally, the body can sustain substantial losses of blood each day for a period of time without ill effects simply because there is a reserve blood-forming capability to draw on. Similarly, as we know from experiences in surgery, people can live and function reasonably well with one lung, one kidney, a portion of the liver, or even a portion of the brain. When there is a margin of reserve capability, the residual tissues or organs simply step up their activities to meet needs. But, as the margin of reserve vitality or capability decreases due to factors such as malnutrition and aging, the forces for disorganization (disease and malfunction) stand an increasing chance of taking over. Eventually, when the forces for organization are no greater than the forces for disorganization, the break occurs, and death is the consequence. This generalized picture of Nature's operational plan is set forth in Figure 4. For every organism, there are environmental influences or deterrences acting to interfere with or prevent life. There is a kind of manifest vigor or biokinetic force sufficient not only to offset the environmental deterrences but also to pro-

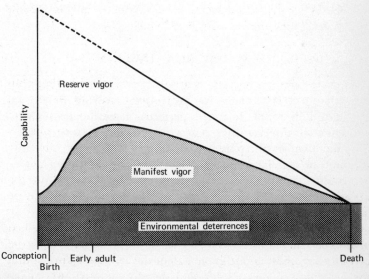

Fig. 4. Elements involved in the life process of organisms.

vide capacity for performance. Beyond this, usually, there is a margin of reserve capability or ecoforce. When the ecoforce, including the biokinetic force, depreciates to a point no greater than the environmental deterrences, death occurs.

Similarly, intellect is also defined as a kind of sustained inter-action—but, in this case, among elements of information, ideas, and concepts instead of the physical elements of nature. Intellect is a kind of sustained interaction in which the power of knowing is offset by the forces causing information to be "garbled" or disorganized. Weak and inaccurate information fed into a computer leads to weak and inaccurate results or conclusions. In computer men's parlance: "Garbage in, garbage out." This principle applies also to the news media, as we know so well, and also to the human mind.

Interplay between the forces for organization and those for disorganization is a generalized process in Nature and, as will be made evident in considerable detail later, underlies operations as significant as evolution and civilization. Identification and evaluation of the determiners of organization, on the one hand, and of those for disorganization, on the other, for whatever process is being considered, will be an investigative approach used in the present analysis. By this means, some additional insight is gained concerning man's paradoxical plight.

OCCURRENCE OF ORGANISMS—INCLUDING LIFE AND INTELLECT

On Christmas Day 1968, Apollo 10 was in orbit around the moon, and by means of newly perfected television-transmitting capabilities, people on the earth were able to see both the earth and the moon in different and revealing perspectives.

From the special vantage point 60 miles above the moon, one could look "downward" at the lunar surface and across the horizon of the moon at the earth as a bright object in the sky. The earth appeared much like the moon has looked as we have observed it over the earth's horizon all during our lives. A common experience previously for many has been to look across the earth's horizon at the brilliant moon and wonder if life existed there.

Now, as we looked "down" at the moon, there were no bright

areas indicating oceans nor any generalized green indicating forests or other plant forms. Indeed, there was no evidence of life. On the other hand, as we looked at planet earth, we knew. There was life on the earth and we wondered why—why organisms, including life and intellect, had arisen on one of these heavenly bodies and not on the other. Some understanding comes from looking more closely at Nature's cavalcade of change as expressed on planet earth. A generalized listing of key events is set forth in Figure 5.

From the existing general knowledge of matter, certain noteworthy deductions can be made.

1. We are aware that the earth is comprised of nearly 100 elements that fit neatly into a Periodic Table of the Elements arranged systematically according to the numbers of protons and orbital electrons. The Periodic Table gives evidence of pattern or system, and the large number of elements with varying potential for uniting in different ways indicates the vast variety of combinations possible.

2. We are aware from incidents in Nature and from experiences in the laboratory that much, if not all, of the materials of early earth existed as gases with the elemental particles in highly randomized motion.

3. We are aware from various experimental and practical

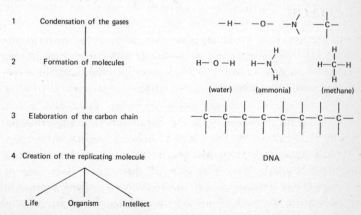

Fig. 5. Key events in the history of planet earth leading to emergence of organisms, life, and intellect.

studies that with time the energy of random movement dissipates through heat loss and radiation, thereby permitting the fast-moving particles to slow down, to come close to each other, and eventually in some cases to unite and form molecules. Much evidence exists indicating that it was by means of steps like these that the substances of the earth were formed and came into being as liquids and solids.

In our listing (Figure 5), we show condensation of the earth's gases as the first noteworthy event in the sequence we have chosen for consideration. Next we show the formation of molecules as a consequence of atomic association and interaction.

Before continuing with the sequence, let us draw still more on general knowledge by taking into account the elements found most commonly in living materials. Outstanding among these are hydrogen, oxygen, nitrogen, and carbon. These are shown at the right in Figure 5 together with the chemical affinity and the valence or combining potential being indicated in each case. Note that hydrogen has a valence of one, which means that it can combine with only one other atom and thus must be at the end of a sequence. In some respects, it is like a period at the end of a sentence. Oxygen has a valence of two and thus can act as a joiner. Nitrogen, in turn, has a valence of three and therefore becomes the basis for branching molecules. Nitrogen has provisional potential. Carbon has a valence of four and becomes the basis for chains, lattices, and matrices. As we know, there are atoms with still other valences and therefore other combining potentials, but it is an interesting fact that the simpler atoms are especially prominent in the materials highly involved in life processes. Radicals or side chains, it may be added, are like adjectives; they give modulation or quality to the condition or action.

Notice (Line 2, Figure 5) what happens when the simplest combinations of the simplest atoms occurs. Some of the most important molecules of Nature's operation on planet earth are formed as a result. Water is one of these, and it is one of the simplest of all molecules. It consists of one uniting atom and two end atoms. It is both an acid and a base, and neutral in terms of acidity. It is a solvent for many types of materials and thus a vehicle or means for many types of chemical processes.

On planet earth, water is abundant, whereas on the moon it is scarce. This difference alone could account for the apparent absence of life on the moon.

Random action, as it appears to have characterized the processes of early earth, has features of importance to developments here. The first formation of molecules such as water, ammonia, and methane, among others, appears to have been occurring only when particular atoms were close enough together and under the right conditions. It is apparent that the occurrence of one type of molecule does not necessarily affect the time of occurrence of the next similar event, but that the availability of molecules does. It follows then that with an abundance of certain types of atoms, a greater abundance of certain types of molecules occurs. In the mix and with time, during the events of early earth, certain exceptional molecules obviously came into existence, or were "discovered" by Nature—molecules that had special capabilities. One of the more important aggregations of atoms thus discovered was carbon linkage; another was the lattice design of the desoxyribonucleic acid molecule, DNA. As now commonly known, the carbon chain became the backbone of the protein molecule so basically important in life processes and DNA became the replicating molecule that provided, and still provides, the basis for organisms, including life and intellect.

With an abundance of certain materials, and with temperature lowering to critical levels, it is likely that some substances like soil and water formed rather rapidly by simple chemical action, including precipitation. On the other hand, for more complex molecules, such as those important to life but without replicating capability, formation probably was much less frequent. Moreover, being isolated and without potential for creating more molecules like themselves, it is apparent that such molecules could not exert any far-reaching influence and in time would disintegrate and disappear. Indications are that there was a long period of geologic cycling of elements and compounds accompanied by a kind of trial-and-error testing of potential of substances formed, leading eventually to DNA. DNA provides opportunity for sustained influence, and by mutational diversity and further trial-and-error testing, for increasing capability and potential. Bearing in mind that there were almost 100 elements available for combination, we can presume that countless "discoveries" were made, only a small portion of which persisted for long or exerted a particular influence. In Figure 5 we show only two of Nature's "discoveries," the carbon chain and DNA. These in time made a great deal of difference in the directions followed by Nature's grand cavalcade of change.

Self-replication, as done by the DNA molecule, marked a turning point in Nature's operational procedures. When certain "raw" materials were available, the DNA molecule "built" them together to form molecules like itself. Its own properties were thus preserved and multiplied. This "discovery" was different from those that had occurred before in that it was not completely dependent on random encounters of particular atoms, radicals, or molecules. When conditions were right, the DNA molecule used the materials at hand and made other molecules with a design like its own. Its influence in a given environment became greater.

Viruses that exist today are related to naturally occurring DNA molecules. They appear to be representatives of the first replicating molecules that came into existence long ago and formed the basis for the emergence of living forms. As we now know, viruses behave, on the one hand, like chemical compounds in that they can be crystallized, and on the other hand, like living objects since under certain conditions they reproduce themselves. For these reasons, viruses can be regarded as a connecting link between the worlds of nonliving and living things.

"Discovery" of the replicating molecule, it now is apparent, laid the foundation for emergence of both life and intellect. Addition of a surrounding membrane with a small amount of protoplasmic medium included transformed the naked DNA into the biologic cell with all its powers of multiplication and growth. Acquisition of the membrane and protoplasm was important in that these entities provided means for performing tasks that could not be performed before, but it was the coming into being of the replicating molecule that made such a difference. DNA became not only the guiding influence in cell performance, but, by means of heredity and other processes, a strong guiding influence in species behavior. Single cells existed as protozoa, and groupings of cells existed as multicellular forms, including human beings. All such forms, single cells and many-celled forms, can receive, process, and utilize information. If we then define life as a sustained physiological interaction and intellect as a sustained mental function, as suggested, we derive impressions of how, by increasing molecular complexification, organisms, life, and intellect came to be over a long period of time (as implied by Figure 5).

ACQUISITION OF POTENTIAL

Increasing molecular complexification involves an important principle and a remarkable and important phenomenology—one significant in the overall cosmologic process operating on planet earth and one which relates to the concept of organization and disorganization. As atoms combine to form molecules, and as molecules combine to form still more complex molecules, new properties are acquired at each step along the way—properties that did not exist before and that are above those of the con-stituent elements combined. Water, for example, has properties quite different from those of hydrogen or oxygen. Water is a liquid, whereas the constituents in free form are both gases. The elements of hydrogen and oxygen through combination become transformed to a new level of functional capability. For our pur-poses, such transformation is identified as *transconstitutiveness*.

Indications are that in Nature's grand plan of operation, trans-constitutive change has been a fundamental feature. The earth, we presume with considerable confidence, first existed mainly as elements which in time combined and then combined addition-ally, gaining transconstitutive properties and capabilities with each aggregation. Some of the newly acquired states, it is ap-parent, were stable and persisted in time while others, for a variety of reasons, were not stable and tended to disintegrate. They lost their organization, reverting to simpler structure or even to the original elements. Again, it appears to have been the margin of difference after the forces for disorganization had acted against those for organization that provides an increment for progress. As we shall see, the principle of transconstitutive transformation will be a factor for consideration over and over again.

NATURAL SELECTION

In the interplay of organization and disorganization, another important principle operates—one well known in biology. It is *natural selection*. In the randomized trial-and-error "testing" inherent in the chance combination of atoms and molecules, some of the newer capabilities fit more naturally than others into given environmental situations. The inevitable competition tended to retain the more stable conditions and reject those less stable. As easily seen, this kind of action comprises the foundation for natural progress. The principle as it operates in living systems is neither humanitarian nor democratic.

ENTROPY AND NEGENTROPY

Another important feature that has a bearing is the tendency of Nature's processes to seek lower energy states. In general, they move toward more stable conditions, giving up energy as they do so. Such action is degradative. In living systems it leads toward death. It is in contrast with the processes that utilize energy, creating a wider margin of reserve vigor and thereby an increased potential for life. Disorganization is an *entropy* process, and organization is a *negentropy* process.

IMPLICATIONS

Important deductions follow from identification of the cosmic events and of the operational principles involved. Two points have been stressed already. One is that the earth is dynamic, is in motion and changing—and has been since the beginning. The other is that because of transconstitutiveness and natural selection, there has been progressive acquisition of operational capability, a significant portion of which has been manifest through living forms.

With respect to progressive acquisition of operational potential as one of Nature's fundamental cosmologic features, emergence of the human mind has particular significance. The mind as the means by which we think, involves brain and it involves memory —stored information. It also involves neural network—circuitry design. The human mind also is a product of transconstitutiveness, natural selection, and progressive organizational design. Because it is one of the latest entities to emerge in the grand progression and because of its vast abilities to comprehend and direct, the human mind can very properly be regarded as evolution's finest product. This is our third deduction.

We return to the question of man's position in Nature's

operational scheme. Man, because of his body design and, in particular, because of his intellect, as has been emphasized, is effective in bringing about change. We then conclude, as our fourth deduction, that *man is Nature's way of achieving accelerated change*. More than any other type of thing that man is doing, he is—we submit—causing change in the overall cosmology.

PERPLEXING QUESTIONS

When one looks at the operation of Nature and man's place in Nature's scheme, as done in this Chapter, some arresting questions arise. One is whether life and intellect were accidents. Attention has been called to randomness as a feature characterizing the processes of early earth at the beginning. Let us suppose that the mix of elements and the chance combinations that occurred had been different from what they were, leaving few or no elements to form water in appreciable amounts, thereby leaving no opportunity for oceans, lakes, or underground streams. Let us suppose also that the carbon chain or the DNA molecule had not been "discovered." Is it likely, then, that life and intellect, as we know them, would have emerged? Are life and intellect in reality only accidents of Nature?

Equally arresting is the question of whether Nature, having forged human life and intellect over such a long period of time, would "permit" them to be swept aside by the unwitting action of man. A provisional and temporarily evasive answer is that, if life and intellect were accidents resulting from chance action of the earth's elements, their disposition could be just as random.

There is another way of asking this central question, however. If the earth was set off with the mix of elements being what it was at the beginning, were life and intellect, as we know them, inevitable? These and matters related will be discussed in chapters to come.

Chapter 3

Systems Models and the Meaning of Brain

A system is a means for accomplishing a task. A chemical process is a means for accomplishing a change in state of elements or compounds. A firecracker or bomb are means for accomplishing explosion blasts. A DNA molecule is a means for accomplishing molecular replication. A biologic cell is a means for accomplishing metabolism and behavior (life). A human being is a means for accomplishing more complex and more intellectual-type behavior—indeed, for accomplishing more rapid cosmologic change on planet earth. Our comprehension and understanding of human beings is enhanced by looking at the character and componency of systems with different levels of complexity.

THROUGH-PUT SYSTEMS

Level 1

Features of systems can be revealed by means of block diagrams. Figure 6 illustrates a simple system. There is input, processor, and output. To be more consistent, one can say input, *through-put*, and output, or sensor, processor, and expressor. Inferences are that something goes into an apparatus, machine, or device and that something comes out in the form of a product, an an-

Fig. 6. Simple through-put system—a reflex. Level 1: cause and effect action.

swer, or a conclusion. A factory is a system for utilizing raw materials and for the production of manufactured items. A radio is a system to receive signals and to produce news and entertainment. An organism is a system for achieving species survival.

Actually, there are many kinds of input, processors, and output as made evident by the following list:

Input	Processor	Output
Raw material	Machine	Product
Signal	Telephone	Communication
Fuel	Furnace	Heat
Stimulus	Cell	Action
Vote	Government	Governance
Information	Brain	Image, concept

The system illustrated in Figure 6 is of the simple through-put type. If it triggers, it fires. When the input is sufficient to start the action, the process carries through to completion—sometimes with great rapidity. The process is reflexive—that is, of the stimulus-response type—and we can refer to it as a *reflex* in order to distinguish it from all other processes that are augmented, modulated, directed, or otherwise controlled.

A reflex with which most people are familiar is the spinal reflex, of which the "knee jerk" is an example. A stimulus just below the knee cap, as input, causes impulses to pass along nerves to and through the spinal cord, as processor, and out along nerves to muscles of the thigh of the same side, causing extension of the leg, as output. The action does not necessitate the use of other parts of the nervous system than those mentioned. The process is that of simple through-put—a reflex. For purposes of reference, we shall identify the reflex as a Level 1 process.

Level 2

A Level 2 process, as classified here, is one augmented and directed toward the achievement of selected goals or objectives (Figure 7). This is accomplished by means of *feedback*, which relates the input to desired output. Consider the problem of heating a room. With a stove, heat is produced, the blaze and the heat varying in a general way with the amount of fuel available to be burned or with the amount of "draft" (oxygen supply). This is a

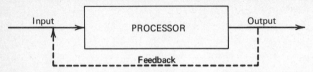

Fig. 7. Through-put system with feedback to provide guidance, balance, direction, and sometimes amplification. Level 2: beginning of automation and self-organization.

simple Level 1 process with input in no way affected by output. With such a system, temperature varies over wide ranges and depends on the attention given to it. On the other hand, if a thermoregulated furnace is used, a fairly even temperature is maintained. This is accomplished by means of feedback involving a sensor or thermostat that detects the level of temperature in the room and transmits appropriate signals back to input in such a way as to regulate the input according to need or goal. When the temperature is slightly low, the input is increased, and when it is slightly high, it is decreased. A thermoregulated furnace or heat source is a Level 2 process.

A steam engine is a beautiful example of a Level 2 process. As the flywheel turns, so also does a governor turn. The governor consists of metal balls arranged to respond to centrifugal force in such a way as to provide feedback control of input steam. As the flywheel tends to turn faster, the balls pull out farther, thereby activating equipment that reduces steam input; as the flywheel tends to turn more slowly, the process works in reverse, feeding in more steam. Depending on design precision, the speed of revolution can be held constant within narrow limits. An automatic pilot operates in much the same way. The plane is set on destination as target (goal) and a gyroscope is employed to detect whether the plane at any given moment is off course. Depending on whether it is veering to the right or to the left, the rudder is operated in such a way as to bring the plane on course again. Regulatory processes also operate in living systems, and temperature control in the human body is a fine example. By means of detector features the metabolic fuel-burning process is regulated according to need in maintaining temperature in a narrow range. Speed of revolution of the flywheel, direction of the plane's movement, and regulation of body temperature are all accomplished by a process of error measurement and correction. Feedback makes this possible. Interestingly and importantly, these kinds of features represent the beginning of automation—meaning control capability within the system. As we know so well, contained control capabilities of every description have been and are employed in living and also nonliving hardware-type systems.

Interestingly and importantly, also, feedback lays the groundwork for self-organization. By means of detectors as sensors, systems obtain information about their environment and about conditions within the system itself. On the basis of the nature of incoming information and the condition of the system as processor, decisions are made and action is taken—often continuously on a moment to moment basis, thus providing behavior. Such action, as we know, takes place in computerized nonliving systems as well as in living systems. Self-organization comprises the basis for behavior.

Level 3

In connection with Level 2-type processes, we recognized automation and self-organization in terms of the capability provided by circuitry and reflex-type through-put action. At Level 3, we add memory, recall, and information-processing capabilities (Figure 8). By memory, we mean storage of information by means of magnetic tapes, discs, and other means as is done in computers and brains of organisms; by recall, we mean retrieval of stored in-

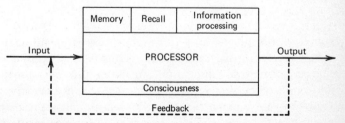

Fig. 8. Through-put system with memory, recall, and information processing, including primitive consciousness. Level 3: beginning awareness.

formation when needed; and by information processing, we mean association of information message elements in such a way as to provide images, concepts, conclusions, or just answers to simple questions. These kinds of facilities are seen in both computerized (nonliving) and living systems. At the third level of systems complexification, quite sophisticated operative behaviors are enabled.

Consider also that in living systems with Level 3 capability there is *consciousness*—awareness. Even in primitive type computers—those with crude sensors—there is "recognition" of features of the environment, a kind of awareness that the environment is different from the "self." Recognition of self, as such, then, is a step only a little more advanced. Whether computers of advanced design have consciousness comparable to that in human beings depends on definitions and premises, but in the context of thinking as developed here, such as possibility becomes difficult to refute.

Consciousness, however, is a unique kind of attribute. There appears to be no consciousness device, as such, but instead it appears to be a culminating capability. When sensor, memory, recall, and association capabilities are provided, consciousness is inherent and appears to be a feature automatically. By the definitions set forth already, it is a transconstitutive capability—one that never existed before and one that suddenly came into being and persisted. Consciousness, as we recognize, is a special attribute. It enables use of the first and second personal pronouns "I" and "you." It causes the system to operate in its own right. It causes the system to have its own interests and concerns. Consciousness was something quite new in the earth's ongoing cosmology.

Level 4

At Level 4 of systems complexification, we recognize three additional transconstitutive capabilities (Figure 9). Whether they came concurrently with consciousness in the evolutionary process or with some additional increase in complexity is not evident as yet, but an answer to this question is not as important as recognition of the potential created by acquisition of the new capabilities. They are instinct, intuition, and emotionality. Instinct is defined as a genetically determined inclination or tendency, intuition as direct perception of "truth" or fact independent of

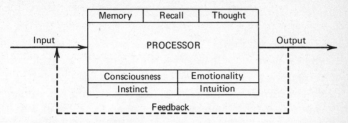

Fig. 9. Through-put system with memory, recall, thought, conscious-ness, low-level emotionality, instinct, and intuition. Level 4: ability to feel and express concern; characteristic of subhuman species.

reasoning processes (immediate apprehension, keen and quick insight), and emotionality as experience and display of feeling such as fear, anger, happiness, contentment, and tolerance. These are capability attributes displayed by subhuman species, par-ticularly those more advanced on the scale of evolutionary de-velopment. Organisms are somehow genetically programmed by nature to function in particular ways in response to certain con-ditions—to perceive and to act purposefully without analysis or reason. In this respect, instinctive and intuitive actions tend to be reflexive in that they are essentially automatic—even though higher levels of coordination than just the spinal cord are in-volved.

Emotionality is a different type of attribute. As a transconsti-tutive capability, it may have arisen concurrently with conscious-ness, instinct, and intuition, or it may have arisen because of them. It is a kind of combined sensing and expression related to "state of being." It makes for mood and personality. Emotionality is displayed by subhuman forms, but not nearly to the extent displayed by human beings.

Subhuman forms are in large degree predictable. They are instinctive, intuitive, and reflexive with respect to survival goals. They respond to hunger by seeking food and to predators by seek-ing shelter. The reactions to stimuli are simple ones—largely of the cause and effect type. Some cunning is displayed by foxes, for example, in turning back on their trails to fool predators and hunters, but this is of low order compared with that of human beings.

Level 5

On the scale of increasing systems complexity, two more trans-constitutive capabilities are added, thus enabling a Level 5 process. They are reason and free will (Figure 10). Reason is a logical analysis-type function and it occurs primarily in the cerebral cortex of the brain. Free will involves the exercise of discrimination and the employment of strategies. These attributes clearly did not arise concurrently with instinct, intuition, and emotionality; they came much later. Human beings operate at Level 5 of the sequence of increasing performance capabilities. Reason and free will are attributes that, in particular, set the human species apart from all others. With reason and free will added to all of the other performance features, a capability was created that generated and advanced civilization, and that caused science and technology to be born and advanced.

THROUGH-PUT SYSTEMS GENERALLY

Systems with differing levels of complexity-enabling processes with increasing functional potential have points in common. All are based on the simple through-put process. All involve goals or purpose. All involve communication, although this is less apparent in simple cause-and-effect processes such as ordinary chemical reactions. All involve power from within or without as input to make the processor operate. All above the level of reflex involve

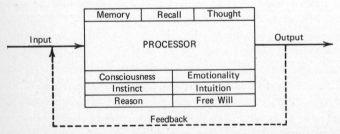

Fig. 10. Through-put system with memory, recall, thought, consciousness, emotionality, instinct, intuition, reason, and free will. Level 5: ability to analyze, and to formulate and employ strategies.

governance, regulation, or guidance. All above reflex involve networks and logic circuits. Most fundamentally, all governance, regulatory, and guidance systems utilize information as the basic commodity. Communication and control comprise the elments of regulation and guidance.

BRAIN AS SUBSYSTEM

The reader will note that in the conceptual design being set forth, we are stressing reflex as the starting point of behavioral and mental functions. This idea is in contrast with an older view that mental function emanates from the brain as a beginning.

If the neural problem or question to be resolved is a simple one, as in case of the knee jerk, through-put is direct and immediate. On the other hand, if it is complex requiring past experience to be brought to bear or requiring the coordinated response of a number of body parts, the input signal is "switched" at neuronal contact points (*synapses*) in the spinal cord and elsewhere as needed, referring the "question" as far "up" through the cord and brain as necessary to coordinate all concerned aspects of memory and circuitry design. According to this picture, reflex is primary and brain is secondary—reflex is system and brain is subsystem. The approach evolves more from the idea of operation than from that of "volume" of mental activity.

Some initiating stimuli, such as a desire or motivation coming from thought, may of course originate in the brain, but this does not prevent the action from being reflexive in basic design. Pure thought occurring only in the brain would be a kind of exception, but even here there is input information, a processing of it, and an output in the form of a conclusion or opinion, thus fulfilling the requirements of basic reflex design.

The reflex process is the basis of digital computer operation and, as we know, a means for accomplishing profound regulation and control action. It is also involved in analogue and many valued logic operations. The reflex process is not necessarily the only basis of "mentative" function in either computers or brains, but it is a basis by which we can better comprehend man, the thinking animal. For the purposes here, *mentation* is defined as *the process of information use*, as done in the mind and to some extent in computers. The *mind* has been defined already as *the means by which we think*; it involves brain, memory, and incoming information.

PHYLOGENETIC PARALLEL

Thus far we have considered the general character of Nature's grand cavalcade of change, and we have discussed systems hypothetically on the basis of increasing complexity. It is impressive and revealing to recognize that in the evolution of species (phylogeny), where communication and control are of such major importance, the acquisition of operative and coordinative potential has followed very closely the steps in increasing complexity and capability described above.

Consider Figures 11 through 15. Figure 11 calls attention to protozoa of which Paramecium is an example. Protozoa are free-living single cells, and they are regarded as one of the most primitive forms of life.

Protozoa are reflexive. They operate as through-put systems in the fullest sense. Under the microscope one can observe the behavior of a paramecium. By means of coordinated lashing of hair-like cilia, the single cell "swims" in a "forward" direction. On occasions, the organism encounters an immovable object, in which case the cilia reverse their direction of beat, the organism backs off and then turns right or left in a meaningful manner. Information is received as input, it is processed within, and logical action as output is the consequence. Requirements for classification as a reflex process are, therefore, fully met.

In tissues, the situation with respect to single cells is the same. In the germinal layer of skin cells, for example, any given cell gets the message from its surroundings as to whether it is to mature and form the tough dry surface cells or simply to proliferate in order to form more cells like itself and thus maintain the germinal layer. A single cell, irrespective of whether free-living

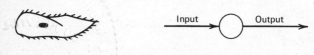

Paramecium

A through-put system

Fig. 11. Single cells. No brain or nerves, as such, but coordinative function.

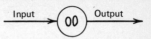

Sea urchin embryo   A through–put system

Fig. 12. Two cells. No nerve fibers.

such as protozoa or contained in a tissue, is a simple through-put information system.

Important to recognize, in passing, is the fact that beautiful and efficient coordinative function is accomplished in single cells without the benefit of nerves or brain, as such. More will be made of this point later.

Figure 12 shows two cells as seen in sea urchin embryos. With normal development, each cell proliferates and in a general way contributes to the overall organism development. If, however, the two cells are separated experimentally with needles, each proliferates to form separate whole organisms—twins. Again, cells, whether singly or as doublets, get the message concerning their immediate environments. Either way, they operate as simple information through-put systems.

Figure 13 shows many cells as seen in the organism volvox, which is barely visible to the unaided eye. In volvox, cells are arranged in a single layer (monoblast) to form a sphere. Each cell has a single hairlike projection or flagellum. These lash in a coordinated way to cause the organism to turn with a rolling movement in the surrounding water. Since coordinated lashing of flagella can be accomplished only with some kind of cell-to-cell communication, it is a reasonable conjecture that such communi-

Volvox   A through–put system

Fig. 13. Many cells in a single layer. Monoblast. No nerve cells, no nerve fibers.

cation occurs. The behavior of volvox as a whole organism is meaningful. It is responsive to its environment and its overall action is purposeful. As a grouping of cells without nerve cells or brain, it is a simple information through-put system, but one involving communication within.

Figure 14 shows the hydra, a *coelenterate*. It is a sacklike organism and consists of two layers of cells—a *diploblast*. In such an organism, simply because of its design, cells in the outer layer (despite evidence of occasional primitive impulse conducting cells) tend to be receptors for information about and coming from the environment; cells in the inner layer function somewhat as expressors—the action takers. There is thus a kind of specialization regarding information handling and action. A division of labor among cells cencerned with communication and control at this level was a new innovation in the progressive development with respect to these functions. In the developments to come, as we know, many kinds of highly specialized sense organs were formed and very elaborate muscle complexes were developed. Actually, the outer cells tend to be contractile also and thus function as expressors as well as sensors. Similarly, the inner cells tend to respond to digestive needs and thus are sensors as well as expressors. At the level of coelenterates, neural function is primitive but there is evidence of emergence of this function. (Cf. T.H. Bullock and G.A. Horriage, *Structure and Function in the Nervous Systems of Invertebrates*, 1965.)

At this stage of the conceptual development, it is important to recognize that most expressor functions of organisms are accomplished by means of muscles—more particularly, groupings

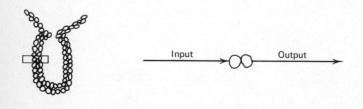

Hydra   A through-put system

Fig. 14. Animals consisting of two layers of cells. Diploblasts. In a general way, the outer cells tend to be receptors and the inner expressors.

of muscles. Locomotion is accomplished by special groups of muscles and so also are facial expression, talking, and swallowing. The one main exception is secretion, which, of course, is accomplished by glands. Expressor functions are muscular functions, primarily.

In diploblasts, cell functions are not very specialized. Nearly all diploblastic cells receive information like sensory cells, conduct stimuli like nerve cells, and contract like muscle cells. The division of labor at this low level of development results almost altogether from cellular locations.

Figure 15 introduces another innovation and again one that appears to have occurred almost incidentally.

The sea walnut, a *ctenophore*, is a triploblast. It also is a sacklike organism but with three layers of cells. Thus, in relation to the outside-inside, sensor-expressor design just described, there clearly are intermediary cells some of which are specialized to function as impulse conductors. In the sea walnut, the intermediary cells are primitive as far as communication and control are concerned, but conducting intermediary cells between cells specialized as sensors and expressors represent the beginning of network and thereby the beginning of brain.

And now let us consider nerve cells, as such. A nerve cell is like other cells except that it has a "hot-line" connection to distant locations. In the lower part of the bodies of human beings

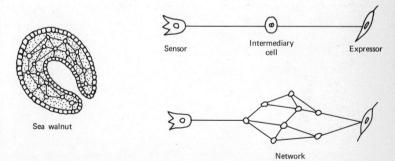

Fig. 15. Animals with inner and outer cell layers and with intermediary cells, involving primitive communicating cells linked as a network. Triploblasts. Primitive neural network and beginning of brain.

—that is, from the waist downward, there are nerve fibers as long as two or three feet, let us say from the spinal cord to the tips of the toes. Nerve cells are therefore specialized for the conduction of nerve impulses. Also, since they have many contact points (synapses) with other nerve cells and since some nerve cells act as stimulators and others as inhibitors of through-put stimuli, they comprise switching mechanisms and logic circuits—in other words: networks.

Figure 16 shows nervous systems as found in widely differing types of animals. Starfishes, in accordance with their radial symmetry, have a neural ring, nerve trunks that extend into the arms, and ganglia (groupings of nerve cells) where nerve trunks connect with the ring. The flatworm, Planaria, with head and tail ends, with rudimentary sense organs, and with mouth parts in the middle rather than the anterior end, has a single ganglion that functions like a brain and branching nerve trunks that con-

Starfish

Planaria

Earthworm

Amphioxus

Fig. 16. Nervous system types showing that arrangement and form correlate with operational needs and developments.

duct stimuli both inward and outward. The earthworm, which is a roundworm with a segmented tube-within-a-tube kind of body arrangement, and mouth, and specialized smell and taste organs at the anterior end, has a double nerve trunk corresponding to the right and left sides; also it has larger ganglia located anteriorly near the specialized sense organs and smaller ones associated with communicating cross nerves at each metameric segment. Amphioxus, a primitive chordate (i.e., an animal with a preliminary backbone) is more strongly cephalized, having as it does sense organs concentrated at the anterior end, a divided but fused nerve trunk with the first three segmental ganglia enlarged. Regarding the early chordate design, there are reasons for believing that the first, second, and third neural ganglia, respectively, were involved with the functions of smell, vision, and hearing.

In the development of individual organisms, as well as in the evolution of species, nerves, ganglia, and brain have been formed and located according to need. This fact helps us appreciate that the nervous system, with all its magnificence and complexity, has developed and evolved in a manner like other organ systems.

PHENOMENON OF BRAIN

It has been indicated that an important kind of information processing is of the digital through-put type, and that with respect to such a system, brain is to be regarded as secondary or subsidiary to the basic reflex. Figure 17 clarifies this. The illustration represents a simple reflex or put-through system with

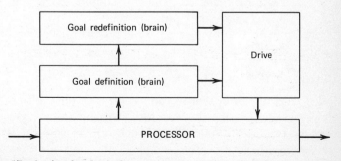

Fig. 17. A simple through-put system with goal definition, goal redefinition, and drive facilities attached.

goal definition, goal redefinition, and *drive* added as special capabilities. The idea is that when an input stimulus seeks expression at through-put and is held in check by some restraining bias or influence, it is referred to goal definition or even to goal redefinition. The outcome results in increased or decreased reinforcement or drive. When sufficient drive is generated, the stimulus is *put through* and, by means of logic circuits, makes its contribution to the behavioral process. When the drive is insufficient to overcome the restraint at through-put, the signal fails, exerting no influence on behavior. This concept of operational behavior would stand as hypothetical, except that it has been tested experimentally. Computers involving this type of design (see Lesti, Human Potential, Volume I, pp. 165 to 177, 1968) are capable of hearing words and answering by means of readout and of doing problem resolution and self-organization tasks of high order, approaching the complexity of tasks accomplished by human beings. Brain as subsystem appears to be a sound concept.

The brain as subsystem contains memory, images, concepts, criteria, standards, ethical values, and moral codes such as those that exist and combine to comprise the overall personality. All of these types of factors, by means of circuitry, are brought to bear on stimuli seeking expression, irrespective of their point of origin —peripheral or from within. Also, by means of circuitry, logic processes are used to obtain the most rational answers compatible with existing standards, values and codes, and to activate muscle group combinations in pattern sequences so as to bring about meaningful behavior.

The point is that digital communication and control processes, despite their beautiful and elaborate symphonic operation, are in basic form (reflex through-put processes) really quite simple, but depending on the complexity of the problem being handled, they may become very involved.

ONTOGENETIC PARALLEL

It has been pointed out that in connection with the evolution of species, there was a stepwise acquisition of communication and control capability corresponding in a general way with the levels of increasing systems process complexity, as described at the beginning of this chapter. Here we wish to indicate a similar parallel in the development of individual organisms (ontogeny).

Multicellular forms start as single cells (fertilized ova, usually). At this stage, their information and control functions, such as they are, are like those of free-living protozoan forms. At the two-cell and many-cell diploblastic and triploblastic stages, the capabilities are similar to those described under *Phylogeny* above. With the formation of cells that act as intermediary to receptors and expressors, nerve cells, network and brain come into being along with increasing behavioral capabilities. The acquisition of functional potential is therefore progressive, leading to increasingly elaborate communication and control function.

Figure 18 is a human neurological development profile of the sort used in the evaluation of brain-injured children. It starts with birth at the bottom and extends upward, covering the first several years of life and showing the expected time of occurrence of different competencies. The three columns at the right show the sensory input functions of visual, auditory, and tactile competence, and the next three columns to the left show the motor (expressor) output functions of mobility, language, and manual competence. The next column to the left shows the age range when the different capabilities are normally expected to appear, and the column next to last shows the portion of the brain primarily involved.

The profile implies that at birth, communication and control functions are accomplished mainly by means of the spinal cord, that at the crawling and creeping stage they are accomplished by spinal cord and midbrain (including pons), and at the stage of walking and talking, by spinal cord, midbrain, and cortex, particularly the latter. This general functional picture has been derived from extensive experimental and clinical tests. In some ways it is an oversimplification but not in general concept. It is a useful basis for analysis.

The profile reveals another important fact—one commonly known, but often overlooked—that neurologic development occurs as a continuum. A fertilized ovum has little intelligence (as normally defined), but a human organism 20 years old, normally, we think of as having a great deal of intelligence. The ability to learn and to know changes a great deal between conception and 20 years of age. Studies reveal that neurological development can be slowed and stopped in many ways, especially by oxygen deprivation; they also reveal that such processes can be

			Expressor or Motor Capabilities		
			COLUMN A	COLUMN B	COLUMN C
Brain Stage		TERM FRAME	MOBILITY	LANGUAGE	MANUAL COMPETENCE
VII	CORTEX	Superior 36 Mon. Average 72 Mon. Slow 96 Mon.	Using a leg in a skill-ed role which is con-sistent with the dominant hemisphere	Complete vocabulary and proper sentence structure	Using a hand to write which is consistent with the dominant hemisphere
VI		Superior 22 Mon. Average 46 Mon. Slow 67 Mon.	Walking and running in complete cross pattern	2000 words of language and short sentences	Bimanual function with one hand in a dominant role
V		Superior 13 Mon. Average 28 Mon. Slow 45 Mon.	Walking with arms freed from the primary balance role	10 to 25 words of language and two word couplets	Cortical opposition bilaterally and simultaneously
IV		Superior 8 Mon. Average 16 Mon. Slow 26 Mon.	Walking with arms used in a primary balance role most frequently at or above shoulder height	Two words of speech used spontaneously and meaningfully	Cortical opposition in either hand
III	MIDBRAIN	Superior 4 Mon. Average 8 Mon. Slow 13 Mon.	Creeping on hands and knees, culminating in cross pattern creeping	Creation of meaningful sounds	Prehensile grasp
II	PONS	Superior 1 Mon. Average 2.5 Mon. Slow 4.5 Mon.	Crawling in the prone position culminating in cross pattern crawling	Vital crying in res-ponse to threats to life	Vital release
I	MEDULLA and CORD	Birth	Movement of arms and legs without bodily movement	Birth cry and crying	Grasp reflex

Fig. 18. Neurological development profile showing normal acquisition of communication and control capability during early life in human beings. Copyrighted by Glenn Doman and Carl Delacato. Reproduced with permission.

stimulated and accelerated by intensified sensory input. Clinical findings show that important gaps or arrests in neurological development may occur and distorting biases may form. Clinical findings also reveal that to a significant degree, gaps can be filled in, inactive neural processes "turned on," and interfering biases overcome by strong sensory programming. Interestingly, these

Sensory capabilities

COLUMN D		COLUMN E		COLUMN F	
VISUAL COMPETENCE		AUDITORY COMPETENCE		TACTILE COMPETENCE	
STEREOPSIS	Reading words using a dominant eye consistent with the dominant hemisphere	STEREOPHONETICS	Understanding of complete vocabulary and proper sentences with proper ear	STEREOGNOSIS	Tactile identification of objects using a hand consistent with hemispheric dominance
	Identification of visual symbols and letters within experience		Understanding of 2000 words and simple sentences		Description of objects by tactile means
	Differentation of similar but unlike simple visual symbols		Understanding of 10 to 25 words and two word couplets		Tactile differentiation of similar but unlike objects
	Convergence of vision resulting in simple depth perception		Understanding of two words of speech		Tactile understanding of the third dimension in objects which appear to be flat
Appreciation of detail within a configuration		Appreciation of meaningful sounds		Appreciation of gnostic sensation	
Outline preception		Vital response to threatening sounds		Perception of vital sensation	
Light reflex		Startle reflex		Babinski reflex	

operational processes apply for computers as well as for human beings.

Ontogenetic development and phylogenetic development parallel each other in the acquisition of communication and control capability, by means of which more options for behavioral function are gained.

MENTATIVE PARALLEL

Still another important parallel in acquisition and use of communication and control capability can be pointed out. If we de-

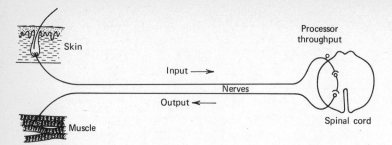

Fig. 19. Spinal reflex with sensory input, processor through-put and expressor output.

1. The reflex is a basic information processing step.

2. It involves sensory input, a processor-through-put, and expressor-output.

3. It involves synapses as switching or decision points.

fine "mentation" as information processing, or simply thought, we can identify it as "mentative parallel."

Figure 19 pictures the simple reflex as it operates through the spinal cord. There is input, through-put, and output. Also, there are synapses as switching points in the spinal cord.

Figure 20 shows the hierarchies of reflex operation required for whole quadruped-type organism coordination. Order 1 is the simple reflex we have been talking about. Order 2 is the same except that output is to the opposite side of the organism as needed when both legs become involved in carrying out a function. Order 3 also starts as a simple reflex, but output extends to a different level as required when arms and hands become involved as well as legs and feet. Order 4 is the same except that output is to the brain in search of goal definition or redefinition. Order 5 is also the same as a reflex in basic design, except that input stimulus originates in the brain and involves any level of expressor function. Actually, Order 5 through-put could operate as a reflex entirely within the brain, and the associative function so characteristic of brain cortex function appears to consist of precisely this type of action. Integration of these different operative reflex functions results in mentation and behavior with all their wondrous manifestations.

Again, the central point is that the basic mentative information process has a design that is simple but may involve processes

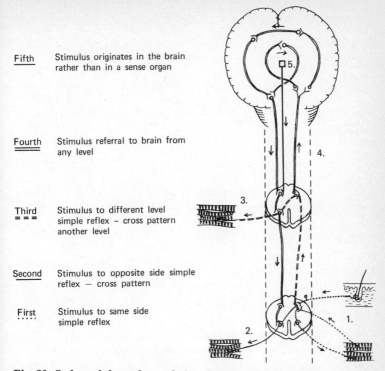

Fifth — Stimulus originates in the brain rather than in a sense organ

Fourth — Stimulus referral to brain from any level

Third — Stimulus to different level simple reflex – cross pattern another level

Second — Stimulus to opposite side simple reflex — cross pattern

First — Stimulus to same side simple reflex

Fig. 20. Orders of through-put; heirarchies of reflex operation.

that are complex. This feature is revealed by each of the parallel operations described.

BRAIN DEVELOPMENT

A significant corollary to phylogenetic elaboration of behavioral capability in higher animal forms has been growth in size of the cerebral cortex of the brain.

In connection with Figure 16, attention was called to the fact that bilaterally symmetrical animals with at least some evidence of backbone in early stages have an elongate nervous system with the three anterior ganglia enlarged to form a forebrain, a midbrain, and a hindbrain, which in a general way have to do with smell, sight, and hearing, respectively. Figure 21 shows how the anterior lobe (forebrain), through phylogenesis—also through ontogenesis—became enlarged and caused to surround and cover

Amphioxus

forebrain | hindbrain
midbrain

Fish

Frog

Cat

Man

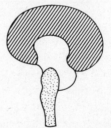

Fig. 21. Phylogenetic and ontogenetic nervous system development.

1. Sensory stimuli arise from sense organs, muscle and brain.

2. Processing involves different levels of nervous system function, depending on needs.

3. Motor responses are accomplished by means of muscles.

the midbrain and medulla (hindbrain). In more advanced forms, nerve pathways lead through the medulla and midbrain (the so-called "old brain") to the cortex or "new brain." The elaboration of cortex has coincided with the acquisition of associative function, including development of images, concepts, and strategies. Associative function is known to be special in the cortex.

A cerebral cortex large in proportion to the rest of the body is a noteworthy feature of human beings.

INFORMATION AND GOAL

Two important deductions follow from our observations about elaboration of brain and the parallels of hierarchical communication and control operations in different kinds of systems: (1) information, as such, is the key ingredient underlying communication and control leading to behavior and (2) systems operations invariably imply purpose or goal. Appreciation of these facts aids in comprehending man's special functional and behavioral capabilities.

Information is an entity apart from the means by which it is processed, the symbols by which it is represented, or even the responses made to it. Messages contain intelligence (dispositional, organized usable and available information), but as such do not themselves as signals constitute intelligence. A road sign, for example, transmits light waves as signals which enter the eye as input, but it is the encoded message of "Stop," "Go," "Turn right," or "Turn left" that is important. The same is true of nerve impulses as signals that travel from the eye to the brain.

Information can be transmitted and stored by means of impulses and symbols, but it exerts an influence only after removal from the encoded signal and interaction with other information occurs, as can happen in a cell, a brain, or a computer as processors. Information is like energy. It moves through devices as systems or processors, causing things to happen as it does. We may ask, in fact, whether information and energy may not in time be found to be interchangeable, similar to the way in which matter and energy are now known to be interchangeable.

Information is a powerful motivator or activator. From moment to moment during any day, it is information coming to us through things said, read, felt, or experienced that to a large degree determines our action. Information is the guiding influence for automation, self-organization, and behavior.

Increasingly, it is recognized that information apart from signals is an entity in its own right, and one that has an attendant system of dynamics of its own. Information is an influence (possibly a force) used in the achievement of organization; it may also be involved in the achievement of disorganization. It has been an influence that has had much to do with emergence of the human species.

Turning now to goal, there are equally significant implications. Before attention was given to feedback and to systems operations as phenomenologies involving fundamental principles and concepts, scientists were reluctant to speak of purpose or goal in connection with the operation of Nature. Purpose sometimes raises the question of omnipotence and scientists of this earlier time simply preferred not to become drawn into a theological controversy where views more than facts were involved.

Governors for steam engines were used well before 1900, and automation involving regenerative electronic circuits were employed and developed enormously just after the turn of the century. Moreover, regulatory processes in living systems were recognized and known about almost since the beginning of biological inquiry. Yet it was not until the early 1940s when feedback and systems as entities were being considered that purpose and goal were forced into the open. A paper published in the journal of *Philosophy and Science*, 1943, by Rosenblueth, Wiener, and Bigelow entitled "Behavior, Purpose and Teleology" marked a turning point. In studies of behavior as the consequence of nervous system function, of control provided by automated devices, and of amplification coming from regenerative circuits, systems as such were found to make no sense except in terms of purpose. From that moment onward, goal has not only been acceptable as a basis for scientific inquiry but it also has been treated as an inherent component for all operational processes as systems.

Clear recognition of goal carries with it an important implication regarding Nature's general system of cosmology. Having spoken of cosmology as a process and having indicated that processes infer goals, we are impelled to ask more insistently what Nature's overall operation is all about.

Cosmology involves two special features. One is randomness of operation and the other is natural selection, both mentioned in Chapter 2. The first, by its nature, involves change; and the second, by its nature, entails a culling out of the less efficient operations. Together random interaction and natural selection promote change with improvement of operational efficiency— seemingly as a goal. At the present stage of understanding, the goal of cosmologic operation appears to be that of improving operational efficiency simply for the sake of improving it, all of which leaves a very open-ended picture, but one enormously important to human beings. Within the limits of this situation is the opportunity for man to direct the course of nature for his own ends—man's omnipotent power, as mentioned in Chapter 2. As we shall also see, there are at the same time some odd prospects for overcoming the human dilemmas. The directions to be taken by cosmologic processes in the future are, to a considerable degree, within the limits of comprehension by the human mind and capable of management by greater elaboration of the mentative function.

Chapter 4

Emergence of Man as a Creature of Intellect

Thus far it has been recognized that man is the consequence of an evolving system—one that appears to be moving toward higher levels of organization and that is being directed increasingly by man. We started with an awareness that man is a creature of intellect, and we have brought forth reasons for regarding intellect as a consequence of information processing.

Intellect we have defined as the power of knowing, leading to behavior with increased options. Growing intellect, as we have shown, occurred concurrently with increasing complexity of nervous systems. Which may have come first and whether one may have been the consequence of the other, are not yet known. On the other hand, because of the piecing together of a great deal of evidence, much can now be said about man's emergence. The purpose here will be to consider more specifically the conditions and the steps by which man became man in the first place.

Thus far, scientists have looked much more at the occurrence of life and at the evolution of body form than at the emergence of intellect. When dealing with the evolution of body form, the procedure has been to consider heredity and environment as the main molding influences—and indeed the only such influences. In dealing with man as a creature of intellect we are impelled to go beyond form and structure and raise the question of whether the conditions and changes seen can be accounted for adequately by heredity and environment alone.

In connection with Level 5 through-put systems, Figure 10, we noted the growing acquisition of communication and control functions—mental powers—and the fact that reason and free will, with their resultant capabilities, are the features that set the human species apart. In Figure 16, attention was directed to various features in evolutionary development, but with stress on the idea that nervous-system design tends to be in accord with the needs of organisms as they are designed and as they function in particular environments. Moreover, we pointed out that, as evolution has occurred, the size of the cerebral cortex has become larger in proportion to the remainder of the body.

Man is a creature with a backbone—one with an internal skeleton and a vertebral column—and it is clear that he arose from other creatures with backbones. In connection with our thesis, the need is to know as much as possible about how intellect first came into being and then about how reason and free will came to be added to animals with backbones that to some extent were already advanced in mentative capabilities.

HEREDITY

Vertebrates, as the immediate ancestors of man, first of all were bilaterally symmetrical. They had right and left sides, They had a front and a back; and they had a head end with concentration of sense organs anteriorly and a tail end. They also had four appendages and tended to walk upright. All these things were provided by heredity. They were inherent in the hereditary design prior to the emergence of man.

There were also other features: the eyes, in contrast with those of fish, birds, and certain other forms, focused on the same field of vision; they were bifocal. Similarly, the arm and leg appendages, in contrast with the leg appendages of horses or camels, say, had the primitive number of five toes and fingers at the end, and with a tendency for the great toes and thumbs to be set off. Finally, the lungs, vocal apparatus, and mouth parts were such that sound utterances could be modulated to make meaningful sounds.

There are, of course, other structural features provided by heredity that could be mentioned, but the ones listed are sufficient for the purposes here. They characterize man's immediate ancestors and they characterize man as he exists at the present time, but by themselves they do not account for man as a creature of intellect.

ENVIRONMENT

In the next chapter, more will be said about the environment in which man arose, but here there is need to account for those elements or aspects that conceivably could have contributed to emergence of a thinking animal.

Anthropological and other evidence indicates that some of the earliest forms of human beings lived in central and southern Africa—also that they lived in the open rather than in forests, mountains, underground, in water or in the air. Evidence also indicates that in central and southern Africa at this early time, temperatures were intermediate rather than extremely hot or extremely cold, that rainfall was suitable for vegetative growth, and that food in the form of plant and animal materials was available in some degree. The African plains and low country thus tended to favor animals that had keen vision, that could stand tall, that could move about with agility, and that had the dexterity, cunning, strength and aggressiveness to protect themselves. We could say, therefore, that what appears to have been man's ancestral environment tended to select for dexterity, mental agility, and performance efficiency—all of which species man came to have—but the same could be said with respect to all environments in relation to any species, thus making it necessary to explore further.

OTHER ELEMENTS

Prior to the period of man there were monkeys, apes, and other animals, mainly in the forests, that under certain circumstances assumed an upright posture, and had the eyes located in such a way that both focused on the same field. Certain of these creatures also had agile fingers and some semblance of an opposing thumb. Some of them were even able to communicate through the use of meaningful sounds made by vocal cords. Man in the open land areas away from forests and aquatic environments somehow went farther in developing functional capabilities. We shall now consider some of the factors that appear to have made a difference, keeping in mind the question of whether it was heredity, environment, or some other kind of influence that made the main difference.

Upright Stance

Although various other animals stand upright in some degree (birds, bears, monkeys, gorillas, chimpanzees), only man has done so to the extent of freeing the forelimbs completely from involvement with balance and locomotion. This made a difference much greater than one at first might expect.

From the standpoint of balance, support of the body on four legs is simple compared with that of support on two legs—especially when locomotion is provided for at the same time.

Body balance is accomplished in part by means of a special sense called *proprioception*. Proprioception is accomplished in part by special sense organs located in muscles and tendons and others in the *semicircular canals* associated with the inner ear. It is difficulties in the latter that account for the condition of *vertigo* or dizziness involved in problems of balance. Nerve stimuli as sensory input coming from the different locations contain information about the degree of muscle tension and about body orientation in space. Such stimuli seek processor through-put but because of their nature are of necessity referred to higher levels in the hierarchial system (Figure 20) and because of their multiplicity and complexity are referred to the highest level—the Order 5 described in Chapter 3. Order 5 of the nervous system through-put operation, as we have pointed out, is largely associative in character, leading to images, concepts, and behavioral patterns. Proprioception is mainly an associative cortical function. In man, where the proprioceptive function is greater, the level of cortical function is correspondingly greater.

Binocular Vision

In animals, such as fish, most of the birds, and many mammals, the eyes are located with one on the right side and the other on the left side of the head. This arrangement has both advantages and disadvantages. It is advantageous because a greater field of vision is involved and disadvantageous because of reduced opportunity for depth perception—that is, three-dimensional (3-D) relationships. Distance can be sensed in two ways (muscle tension required in focusing the lens and scope of the field under view) and both can be accomplished by the eyes singly. When the two eyes are focused on the same object, a sense of three-dimensional relationships is obtained by the muscle tension required to turn the eyeballs inward in case of near objects and to turn them outward for far objects.

Visual Convergence

Turning the eyeballs inward or outward and the attendant lens adjustment required to focus on near or far objects is called *visual convergence*—a function that goes hand in hand with binocular vision. For certain kinds of organisms, near point convergence (say, to within six to twelve inches) is not nearly as important as for others. A fox or mountain lion looks ahead to where the prey or predators are and a horse or dog looks ahead to where they are going. Rarely is the vision of quadrupeds fixed on the forelimbs or front feet. A human being, in contrast, so very often is looking at objects he is manipulating with his hands, often within a few inches of his eyes. Visual convergence of necessity goes along with manipulative skills. It is a complex coordinative function and thus involves the cerebral cortex to a large degree.

Brachiation

The ancestors of man who lived in trees of the forests, quite obviously used their upper appendages for grasping, hanging, and swinging—types of functions aided by flexibility of the fingers, agility of the hands, multidirectional movements of the wrist, and twisting or rotational movements of the forearm. All such functions, it is apparent, were forerunners for or comprised a foundation for the manipulative skills that emerged later in species man.

Prehensile Grasp—Supination and Pronation

With upright stance the forelimbs were relieved of mobility functions and thus were available for other uses. The forward appendages of human beings, and to some extent of other primates, have anatomical features that enable them to manipulate objects in a way that would be impossible for horses or seals, for example.

The first anatomical feature was having the thumb set off from the first finger in such a way as to enable grasping. Not only could the thumb and fingers be wrapped around objects in opposite directions, but also the tips of the thumb and first finger could be used to pick up small objects—even small objects such as leaves, sticks and even grains of sand with use of the finger nails. Squirrels, as we know, sit or stand upright and skillfully manipulate objects with their forelimbs. They do this mainly by holding the objects between the two paws or hands, and thus lack the agility of manipulation with a single paw or hand.

Second, the bones of the wrist and elbow became arranged in such a way that the hand could be rotated. The palm could be turned upward or downward—*supination and pronation*, respectively. The twisting capability, combined with that of grasping, permits skills such as turning a screwdriver, placing a nut onto a bolt, and putting a cap onto a jar. In terms of muscles, joints, and bones, the forearm and hand are extremely complex. Their guidance and control involve coordinative cortical function of high order.

Truncal Rotation

Upright posture enabled still another important capability. This was the twisting of the body—*truncal rotation*. In four-footed animals with the body mostly in horizontal orientation, twisting truncal movements are difficult and not much in evidence. In animals that stand upright and therefore in a posture favorable to twisting movements, body rotation assumes major significance. Consider, for example, the discus throw, the golf swing, the baseball pitch, the tennis serve, and the bowling throw. Think how ineffective these functions would be without truncal rotation. Acquisition of the simple feature of body twisting made a great deal of difference in performance capabilities. It also required a much more advanced coordinative function.

Consideration of the muscle groups involved in truncal rotation reveals just how extraordinary the coordinative function actually is that can bring off "a hole-in-one" in golf, a sequence of "strike-outs" in baseball, and a pattern of "strikes" in bowling. Study of embryology reveals that the primitive muscle design for verte-brates is muscle arrangements for each vertebra or body segment, much as exists presently in fish. With development of append-ages, certain of the primitive segmental muscles—or myotomes, as they are called—became altered to provide the groupings needed for leg movements. Then, with upright posture and the needs for body twisting in the performance of work skills (chopping, hammering, sawing), as well as performance of the athletic skills already named, there was need to involve very large complexes of muscles—groupings which, in the quadruped, rarely functioned together. Truncal twisting movements are accomplished by lines of pull that extend diagonally and upward around the body across the abdomen, and through the back and neck to the head. Coordination and sequential timing of such groupings required neural control well above the levels of spinal cord or old brain (diencephalon or midbrain).

Sidedness and Cerebral Hemispheric Dominance

Generally, it is appreciated that individual human beings tend to be right- or left-handed, as the case may be; but, not as well appreciated is the fact that individuals tend also to have "eyedness," "earedness," and "footedness." Choice of hand with which to manipulate, choice of eye with which to sight, choice of ear to cock in detecting the source of sound, choice of foot with which to kick a football, and choice of words with which to begin a sentence are necessary for smooth behavioral functions. Failure to make a choice easily and efficiently results in awkwardness and stammering.

One concept is that all functions measured by the Neurological Development Profile, Figure 18, "are considered to have attained the uppermost level of neurological organization when the cortex of one cerebral hemisphere is dominant in the control of their performance." Clinically, it has been observed that "in the finer degrees of their execution, these skills are most commonly accomplished in normal individuals by the consistent use of one eye, one hand, one foot and one ear in the dominant role" (LeWinn, *Human Neurological Organization*, Charles Thomas, 1969).

Sidedness in neural control is made very evident in cases where a heavy blow is sustained on one side of the head, resulting in paralysis on the opposite side of the body.

In a right-handed person, under normal circumstances, the right hand takes the action and the left hand serves the right. The left hand holds the paper while the right hand uses the scissors to do the cutting, and the left hand holds the needle while the right hand manipulates the thread to accomplish the threading.

Question is thus raised as to whether in the upper reaches of cortical function, as occurs in human beings, one cerebral hemisphere sets the line of sight and develops and keeps fixation on the objectives while the other concerns itself more with measurement of error, determining how much the action is off course, and so on. Hemispheric dominance is understood in very limited degree thus far, but its existence and the need for dominance in decision making are fully evident. One of the fascinating questions inherent is why control functions can be performed better by two computers working side by side than by one with adequate capacity.

We are now aware, from the features mentioned thus far, that simple anatomical changes like upright posture, the opposing thumb, the rotating forearm, and the bifocal eye arrangement, by their presence, opened the way for greater performance potential—that is, when accompanied by adequate control potential. Such anatomical features, including the brain capacity for coordination, could have been provided by mutations in the chromosomal materials of heredity. More insight is obtained, however, by recognizing still other kinds of developmental changes.

Use of Tools and Weapons

Very early, human beings learned to use implements. With the hind or lower limbs totally adequate for locomotion, with arms and hands available for manipulation, with hand-eye coordination of high order, and with increasing guidance, planning, and control capability in the brain, human beings began to use bones, stones, sticks, and even fire as aids both for protection and for hunting. Used in a primitive way, implements constituted only slight advantage, but in time man thought of ways to break bones under twisting stress to obtain sharp points, and of ways to shape stones to obtain cutting edges. With the availability of tools and weapons, planning and strategy use in the hunt or in fending off enemies became increasingly important. There were increasing demands on the mental powers, especially those of the associative and integrative types. In more practical terms, there was more of a need to measure, to quantitate, to compare, to evaluate, to make records, and so on—the kinds of things that depend on language and communication.

Abstractions, the Use of Symbols, and the Invention of Language

With the use of tools and weapons proving ever more advantageous, and with strategy planning becoming increasingly important, there was increasing need for communication. It is understandable that certain vocal sounds came to be used early for warning purposes and that gestures of particular types came to connote the need for action. However, it was a large and much more significant step mentally to think of using shapes (characters or letters) and sounds (words to represent names of things (nouns). It was still a greater step to use words (verbs) to provide action, and other words (adjectives, adverbs, and articles) to provide quality, tone, color, and degrees of modulation. Development of language, although it may have occurred slowly, was a transconstitutive mental step of first magnitude. With language skills, human beings functioned at higher levels of performance capability and with new levels of comprehension and awareness.

Some animal species developed specialized olfactory organs and followed scent trails. Early human beings, with keen vision, followed tracks. But tracks are not animals. They are representative of animals. They therefore, are abstractions. Although being apart from animals (friend or foe), tracks were thought of in connection with animals. With new abilities in mental visualization, primitive human beings by means of their eyes learned not only to understand that a particular type of animal had been where the tracks were, but that it traveled in a particular direction. In our own time, seeing and interpreting in two dimensions seems such a simple matter, but since no other species apart from man has developed this ability, it must necessarily be regarded as a major mental achievement; and, as we know, this innovative development laid the foundation for many others.

Quantitation, Art, and Ritual

Systems of counting were also needed by early man. By using pebbles or fingers to represent objects and by moving one each time one of the objects moved past a certain point, a method was devised for keeping count. This was a one-to-one correspondence abstraction and it became the basis for many complex and powerful mathematical procedures. Art and rituals are also forms of abstractions, and their use by human beings is much more prevalent than use by other animal types. Abstraction as a special capability relates to still other emerging capabilities.

Emotionality

The ability to experience and to feel emerged and evolved along with other capabilities. Fear, anger, and contentment are expressed by subhuman forms as well as human, but the ability to respond emotionally to the conditions of life is stronger and more advanced in human beings. Expressions of love and hate can become intense beyond reason or rationality in human beings and, not infrequently, human beings will lay down their lives because of feelings about fairness and the principles of right or wrong.

Consider especially the emotionality of sex-love. The exhilaration, commitment, and satisfaction that comes to human partners is exceptional and obviously beyond that of most if not all other species. This capacity is provided in part by certain anatomical and physiological features, but there is also the question whether the larger cerebral cortex and the greater associative mental functions in man do not contribute to greater emotional capacity. The opportunity to develop higher levels of sexual response is enhanced in human beings for several reasons: greater skin sensitivity over the entire body; the use of lips and fingers for purposes of stimulation; and the fact that in human beings sexual participation is not confined to a particular season of the year nor to particular parts of an estrus cycle. As is evident, a cerebral function is required in addition to make the greater emotional experiences possible.

Implications are therefore that man's increasing mental capability provided or enabled greater emotional capabilities as well as others.

Logic and Reason

Emergent quite clearly along with advanced cortical functions has come the ability to employ *logic* and *reason*, to employ induction and deduction—indeed to interrelate rationality. Human beings, out of a desire to have complete concepts, fill in with fictional and imaginary ideas where there are gaps in knowledge.

Such ideas, after being carried along as folklore or myths for a period of time, come to exert an influence. As examples, consider fairies, the Easter bunny, Santa Claus, angels and Satan. Beyond these tendencies, however, through exploration and investigation, human beings have learned more about the laws and the realities of Nature, and thus have come increasingly to conduct themselves in accordance with the realities and to behave in a more rational manner.

Free Will

Also appearing along with advanced associative functions has been the ability to develop and to utilize strategies—to plan, to scheme, to exercise cunning, and to discriminate. A fox may double back on its trail to deceive the hounds and the mother bear may lead hunters away from her cubs, but only human beings develop business strategies, social reforms, and international treaties.

The behavior of a subhuman animal is reasonably predictable. When hungry, he will seek food; when in danger, he will take cover; when threatened, he will fight; and when sexually desirous, he will seek a mate. Human beings, on the other hand, may look ahead to a more favorable outcome in the end and at any given time do other than what would be expected as a direct answer to a need. With all its ramifications, *free will* by itself would be sufficient to set the human species apart from all others.

HIERARCHIES OF INTELLECT

Inherent in the brief treatises on "Other Elements" is an implication—that there are levels or hierarchies of mental capability as well as levels of through-put systems capability and levels of nervous system function, and that the different levels of mental capability arose sequentially in time.

Table 1 presents thoughts on the emergence of intellect, which carry with them the idea that as one level of intellectual innovativeness was achieved, it formed a groundwork for achievement of the next. The left column shows the structural entity involved; the second column indicates the intellect capability of each structure with acquisition of capability shown as sequential and progressive; and the third column is the function of each level.

Table 1. Emergence of Intellect (Underlying Transconstitutive Steps).

Structural Entity	Intellect Capability	Function
DNA	Molecular properties	Replication
Cell	Metabolism	Self-powered reacting device
	Reflex	Primitive information processing
Organism (Many celled)	Memory	Information storage
	Consciousness	Awareness of self and environment
Human being	Curiosity	Desire to know
	Intuition	Immediate apprehension; reflex through-put process
	Imagination	Tendency to fill gaps in knowledge (even with unreliable facts and data)
Modern man	Reason	Acceptance that nature "plays fair" and that actions and reactions are in agreement with "natural laws"; assumption that the facts of Nature are verifiable; scientific method; hypothesis and test.
	Rationality	

This table represents the sequential picture that is obtained when account is taken of the occurrence of new and innovative mental functions in relation to development. It emphasizes the idea that intellect, the same as body form, has been emergent in time and did not just appear full blown at some particular moment, a matter not much considered heretofore.

INFORMATION AS THE COMMODITY OF MENTAL FUNCTION

The question to which attention is being directed in this chapter is that of how intellect came into being in the first place and then how reason and free will, the features that set the human species apart, came to be added.

In classical biology, the view is that heredity and environment, and only heredity and environment, are the determiners of species types. After indicating the elements of heredity and environment that obviously had a bearing, a substantial list of "Other Elements" was set forth which clearly have had a strong influence. The list of other elements included a proportionately larger brain, upright stance, binocular vision, visual convergence, prehensile grasp, supination and pronation, truncal rotation, sidedness in neurological control, cerebral hemispheric dominance, use of tools and weapons, use of symbols as abstractions, language, quantitation, art and ritual, emotionality, logic and reason, free will, and hierarchies of intellect.

Emergence of a larger and more advanced cerebral cortex—meaning its physical and structural aspects—conceivably could have occurred as the consequence of mutation and selection. So also might the opposing thumb, the rotating hand, and the associated eyes. Likewise, the surrounding environment could have, and obviously did provide the ecologic niche into which more advanced thinking organisms could fit and live. But, what about the actual grasping action and the actual hand rotation, both of which are carried out only with neural control? Where did the learned coordinative procedure come from? What about truncal rotation that is accomplished with existent muscular groupings coordinated and integrated in a different kind of way? What about the use of tools, weapons, fire, and abstractions—features that seemingly contributed greatly to the emergence of intellect? Did such elements as part of the environment exert an influence, or was it a matter of experiencing them that made a difference? What about consciousness, intuition, emotionality, hemispheric dominance, logic, reason, and free will—attributes that somehow act to determine character but that come from within? Can the mental development stemming from such influences be said to come from either heredity or environment? What about the hierarchies of intellect? Can they be said to have been induced by either heredity or environment?

Here it must be recognized that the innovative capabilities of higher forms came from two kinds of development. One was formation of the specialized organs by means of which the newer kinds of action could be taken, and the other was formation of communication and control capability in the neural network and brain sufficient to coordinate and bring off the more advanced functional action. Changes thus had to occur at about the same time in a properly related way in different organs, including bones, joints, muscles, nerves, and brain. It is also important to remember that *information is the commodity of communication and control operations*—of neural network and brain. Underneath many, if not all, of the molding influences mentioned above is information, which ebbs and flows, working its influence as it does so. Underneath also was information processing as a molding factor.

Here, we employ the term *"mentation"* in referring to the processes of information use, or simply the processes of thinking, as done in the nervous system (including the brain), and as done in a related way in computers.

The questions being considered involve mentation and mind as well as heredity and environment.

INFORMATION GENERATIVENESS

Still another feature important to recognize is that *information interacting with information is generative*. In the brain, and particularly in the cerebral cortex, information interacts with other information (the associative function) to create new information —ideas, answers, images, and concepts that never existed before. Such newly created information is stored immediately and it begins at once to exert an influence on other information and therefore on the behavior of the organism with which it is associated. *Information is the commodity of mentation and mentation is the basis of learning, programming, and conditioning which, in turn, comprise the basis of specialized behavioral function.*

MENTATION AS DETERMINER

Allowing for the idea that information interacting with information is generative, it follows that the enlarged brain, with its associative functions, became not only a source of new information and thereby an influence on developmental behavior, but also an innovator by means of which new developmental and behavioral potential was created.

In a previous article (*Human Potential*, 1, 99–106, 1968) I have questioned whether, because of the special conditions associated with the emergence of intellect, it is necessary to consider a third influence—namely, mentation (information processing)—as an element along with heredity and environment acting to mold species types.

Energy, as we have seen, is an ingredient of action, and this is true irrespective of whether the action is purposive. Information is also a strong motivator in purposive systems. It initiates and sustains action. When we stop to think of it, it is apparent that our individual actions from moment to moment of every day are largely determined by information coming into our bodies from the environment more or less continuously through sense organs. To a large degree, it is what we see, hear, feel, and sense that initiates and directs our behavior, and information is the underlying commodity involved.

As we have discussed, the processing of information (mentation) and the acquisition of transconstitutive functional potential have been features in the life process since the "discovery" of the replicating molecule, DNA. Accordingly, since each innovative step has in its way constituted groundwork for the next innovative step, and since intellect appears to build out of information associative experiences (mentation) creating vacuums by generating imaginative ideas and needs, attention has been directed beyond heredity and environment in the usual sense. In time it may become possible to fit the mentative developmental influences (mentation) neatly into the categories of heredity and environment. But, for the time being, it is necessary to regard mentation—the whole domain of information processing—as a new dimension in the field of biology and, at the same time, as a factor that has had much to do with the emergence of man, the creature of intellect.

THE MIND OF MAN

If we define mind as the means by which we think (process information), it obviously consists of a nervous system, including the brain, of information processing potential, of memory, and of judgment capacity—discretionary potential involving reason and free will. Nervous systems are physical. They are comprised of tissues and therefore atoms and molecules, which are substances of the earth. Memory, meaning stored information, consists of message and meaning and, although dependent on physical materials to have a place to reside and interact, is not itself physical. Information consists of facts and data, which are not physical but mental. Information, like energy, is dynamic. Also, like energy, it exerts an influence in systems. Intuition, imagination, and emotionality are features of the information process in living systems. Reason and discretion (free will) are transconstitutive extensions that have reached their highest point of expression in the human species.

Why subhuman organisms do not develop and utilize reason and free will is an interesting question. Obviously, there is mentative capability in the human brain that they do not have, and we are led to ask if the more advanced mental capacity can in reality be attributed to mutation and natural selection—in other words, to heredity. Possibly so, but it is necessary to remember that nervous-system capability tends to develop and distribute according to need, and that mentative function tends to create need, thus making it impossible at this stage to dismiss the information-processing influence.

We leave this subject area, therefore, with the view that the mentative function, along with and integrated with heredity and environment, has been an important determiner of human emergence. To be human means to have intellect, and to have reason and discretion according to certain accepted standards and goals. With standards and goals, a man has character that is uniquely his own. It is the essence of man we speak of as *soul*. Whether the soul—that which is the essence of man—has existence after death of the body will not concern us here.

Chapter 5

Man's Origin, Kinds of Human Beings, and Man's Singular Position

As part of our quest to understand the nature of man and his wending way, it is important to locate species man more precisely in the matrix of time and in the sequential pattern of unfolding events.

TIME DESIGNATIONS

Relating the cosmic events of planet earth in time can be approached and extended in different ways. First, one can set the moment of the earth's origin as time zero and then measure forward in increments of time. Second, one can choose a recent event, such as the birth of Christ, and measure backward in time increments. Neither of these approaches has proved particularly useful or satisfying because of vagueness and lack of knowledge about the time intervals actually involved as the earth came into being. A method frequently employed is one that neglects the uncertain moment of beginning and deals only with that portion of the earth's history that is better understood. This is the method based on geological events, which, of course, began as the earth developed a hard crust at the surface with oceans. Rocks formed at that early time exist even today, and by means of argon dating, uranium-lead ratios and other methods some of which have been mentioned already, reasonably precise estimates have been made of their ages. Rocks formed since have been laid down in layers according to time, and within certain types of layers exist the fossil remains of organisms showing changes as they occurred in time. Studies of rock layering and of positioning of fossil types with respect to each other, have provided information about ages and time sequences, with respect to both geological and biological events.

The accompanying table presents a picture. The figures are from Kulp (*Science* 133: 1105, 1961). They are probably as well substantiated as any that could be presented.

Table 2. Geologic Time Table

Era	Period	Epoch	Beginning of Interval (Millions of Years Ago)
Cenozoic (New Life)	Quarternary	Recent	1
		Pleistocene	
	Tertiary	Pliocene	13
		Miocene	25
		Oligocene	36
		Eocene	58
		Paleocene	63
Mesozoic (Middle Life)	Cretaceous		135
	Jurassic		181
	Triassic		230
Paleozoic (Ancient Life)	Permian		280
	Carboniferous		345
	Devonian		405
	Silurian		425
	Ordovician		500
	Cambrian		600
Proterozoic			1400 (?)
Archeozoic			1850 (?)

Notice that time is designated by eras, periods, and epochs. Notice also that geologic intervals since formation of the earth's crust bear specific names, and that estimates have been made (last column) of when each interval began. Indications are that the earth formed a hard crust and oceans four to five billion years ago, as shown in Figure 1 of Chapter 1, and that the biologic cells came into existence one to two billion years thereafter. On the basis of data as given and of identification of the human species as now defined, man then came into existence during or shortly before the Pleistocene Epoch, which began about a million years ago and extended to about ten thousand years ago.

This means that if geologic time were considered as one day—24 hours—man's interval would be equivalent to less than the last minute.

MAN'S IMMEDIATE ANCESTORS

A question that concerned scientists and others during the last century was whether man arose from existent primate forms such as monkeys, chimpanzees, or gorillas or from some extinct animal form. Without going into detail here with respect to the fossil and anatomical reasons as to why, the best available evidence indicates that man and the other living primates arose from common ancestors that existed tens of millions of years ago (see Figure 22).

By the rules of taxonomic nomenclature, a grouping of organisms can be said to belong to the same species when (1) interbreeding can occur, (2) serological tests on tissue proteins show points in common, and (3) members of the group have certain unique features in common. Assuming capability of interbreeding and proper serological conditions, the unique feature that sets the human species apart, as indicated already, is the ability to think—to exercise advanced powers of intellect, mentation. Just how man is identifiable as a species becomes more understandable by considering the usual rules of nomenclature.

According to classification procedures commonly used, organisms are designated by phylum, class, order, family, genus, and species. First, man is a member of PHYLUM *Chordata*, that large grouping of animals with internal skeletons usually with vertebrae. Man is also a member of CLASS *Mammalia*, consisting of animals with warm blood and that suckle their young; of ORDER *Primate*, involving forms that are proficient in the use of hands and brains; FAMILY *Hominidae*, comprised of manlike creatures that walk on two feet; of GENUS *Homo* meaning man, on the ground, with communication by means of language; and, finally, SPECIES *sapiens* meaning wise ones—hence *Homo sapiens*—thinking animals. Man is identifiable in particular by his advanced powers of intellect and by the use of articulate speech. Man is the only creature to communicate by means of a language. A quick and easy way to characterize man is to say that he is a creature that walks upright and talks. Both walking upright and

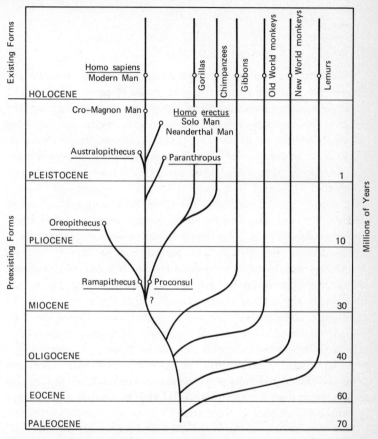

Fig. 22. Evolutionary lineage suggesting that man and other existing primates arose from common ancestors (adaptation from LIFE, *The Epic of Man*, 1961, p. 13).

communicating by means of speech, as we have seen, involve advanced cortical functions.

NUMBER OF HOMINOID SPECIES

Fossil evidence is scanty, at best, but a sufficient amount is available to show that a number of kinds of creatures existed during the early Pleistocene Epoch that walked upright and had larger brains (see again Figure 22). One by one each became extinct, however, except *Homo sapiens*. Man stands alone as a creature of advanced intellect.

MAN'S PLACE OF ORIGIN

The remains of humanoid creatures that existed during the early Pleistocene have been found in a number of parts of the world.

There were the bones of Neanderthal Man found first in Germany and then across Southern Europe, Southern Asia, and Northern Africa; there was Cro-Magnon Man whose bones were found first in France and then across Southern Europe; there were Peking Man and Solo Man whose bones were found, respectively, in China and Java; and there was the man-ape, *Australopithecus*, whose bones were found in South Africa. All these types of creatures, as well as other man-like forms not mentioned, lived during the middle or early Pleistocene Epoch, 500,000 to 1 million years ago. Although reasonably precise dates have been established for the time when each type of fossil man existed, this information in itself does not indicate whether the specific individuals whose bones were being studied occurred early or late in the history of its species type. A knowledge of developmental relationships and especially of skeletal anatomy was required for decisions on such matters and, when applied, it was apparent that the Southern Ape was definitely the older and could well have been a representative of or near relative of the heretofore missing link between man and his earlier Primate ancestors.

There is thus a growing body of evidence that species man first existed on the open savannas of South Africa. It is necessary to recognize at the same time, however, that there are lingering questions as to whether creatures that walked upright and talked might not have arisen from different primate stocks at different times and at different places in the world. Growing impressions are, nevertheless, that species man emerged from a single primate type or certain closely related types that existed in Africa about 750,000 years ago and that *Australopithecus* was either a direct ancestor of man or a close representative. Certain well-reasoned speculation has been that man, adapted as he was for walking, was not well enough suited for life in the forests to compete successfully against other primate groups there, and thus was forced onto the open savannas.

RACIAL TYPES AND THEIR MIGRATIONS

As is commonly known, many types of human beings exist on the earth at the present time. There are groups that are tall and others that are short; there are groups that have high cheek bones and others that have low cheek bones; there are those with straight black hair and those with wavy blond hair; and there are also those that have light skin color while others have dark skin. From the standpoint of classification, any combination of factors can be used to identify and to designate different groups. Geographic location, body type, and skin color have all been used. The accompanying classification list is one set forth by Dobzhansky in *Mankind Evolving*, 1962. It recognizes 34 human types, and the number of course could be larger or smaller depending on kinds of classification criteria employed.

By looking at the multiplicity of types of human beings existent at the present time, one can understand why questions have arisen concerning multiple origins. However, the differences that exist can be accounted for, reasonably, it would seem, by mutation and natural selection, including sexual selection. By spontaneous mutations induced in part by the ubiquitous earth radiation, a diversity of types of organisms come into existence. This is Nature's way. Then, by means of survival-of-the-fittest procedures automatically inherent, those organisms better adapted to survive in particular environments are retained to reproduce their kind. Additional isolation is obtained by inbreeding because of the tendency of individuals to mate with other individuals having characteristics similar to their own. During the period of modern man—say, the last 200,000 years—many kinds of human beings have come into existence as indicated in some degree by the Dobzhansky chart.

An intriguing question, which now emerges, is how human beings, assuming they arose from a single source, became distributed around the earth. Figure 23 presents some ideas.

Man, as we have noted, tended to live in the open and to move about in search of food. It is natural that he would go where the hunting was best, and it follows that through time migration occurred somewhat randomly, that individuals lived and died as

Chart 1. Classification of Human Beings by Location and Features

Northwest European	Scandinavia, northern Germany, northern France, the Low Countries, U. K., Ireland
Northeast European	Poland, Russia, most of Siberia
Alpine	From central France, south Germany, Switzerland, northern Italy, eastward to the Black Sea
Mediterranean	Both sides of the Mediterranean, from Tangier to the Dardenelles, Arabia, Turkey, Iran, and Turkomania
Hindu	India, Pakistan
Turkic	Turkestan, western China
Tibetan	Tibet
North Chinese	Northern and central China and Manchuria
Classic Mongoloid	Siberia, Mongolia, Korea, Japan
Eskimo	Arctic America
Southeast Asiatic	South China to Thailand, Burma, Malaya, Indonesia
Ainu	Aboriginal population of northern Japan
Lapp	Arctic Scandinavia and Finland
North-American Indian	Canada and the United States
Central-American Indian	From southwestern United States, through Central America to Bolivia
South-American Indian	Agricultural Peru, Bolivia and Chile
Fuegian	Nonagricultural areas of southern South America

the migration occurred, and that evolution by mutation and natural selection took place while these things were going on. With such procedures in progress, it would have been natural for factions with particular traits to become isolated in pockets here and there in different parts of the world, and this appears to be precisely what happened.

Starting in South Africa, any land migration of necessity would have to be northward. The Mediterranean area, having a temperate and semitropical climate, was favorable for man's type of life. Early fossil remains of human beings have been found at various places around the Mediterranean Sea and eastward in Asia.

The Pleistocene Epoch, it should be remembered, was a glacial

Chart 1 (continued)

East African	East Africa, Ethiopia, a part of Sudan
Sudanese	Most of the Sudan
Forest Negro	West Africa, much of the Congo
Bantu	South Africa, part of East Africa
Bushman and Hottentot	South Africa (aboriginal inhabitants)
African Pygmy	African equatorial rain forests (small-statured people)
Dravidian	Southern India and Ceylon (aboriginal populations)
Negrito	Philippines to the Andamans, Malaya, and New Guinea (small-statured and frizzly haired populations)
Melanesian-Papuan	New Guinea to Fiji
Murrayian	Southeastern Australia (aboriginal population)
Carpentarian	Northern and central Australia (aboriginal population)
Micronesian	Islands of the western Pacific
Polynesian	Islands of the central and eastern Pacific
Neo-Hawaiian	Hawaii (an emerging population)
Ladino	Central and South America (an emerging poulation)
North-American Colored	North American (negro)
South-African Colored	South Africa (negro)

period. There were ice sheets in Northern Europe and Asia which, it appears, tended to hold back human migrations inasmuch as there is little evidence of human fossil remains where the ice sheets existed. Neanderthal and Cro-Magnon men seem to have existed throughout the Mediterranean region, and factions probably more closely related to Cro-Magnon man across Southern Asia through Malaysia to Java and possibly Australia. Another faction migrated into China, and still another across the Bering Straits to North and then to South America, the latter being ancestors of the American Indian.

In time, Neanderthal Man became extinct, leaving Cro-Magnon Man—and possibly other groups, although this is now doubtful. Although racial origins are not at all clear as yet, it is evident that factions of black men developed in Africa, factions of white men developed in Europe, and factions of brown men

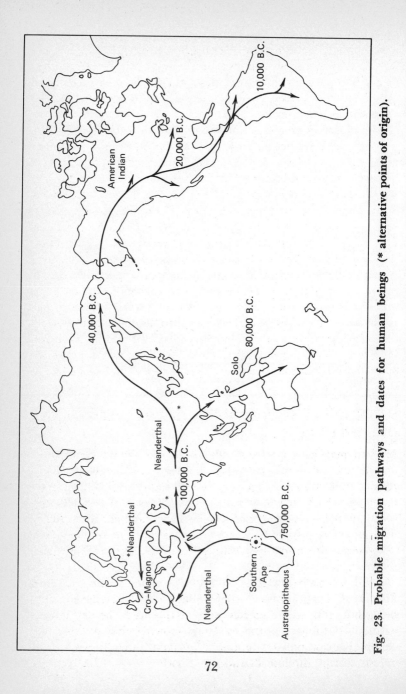

Fig. 23. Probable migration pathways and dates for human beings (* alternative points of origin).

American Indian

20,000 B.C.

10,000 B.C.

40,000 B.C.

80,000 B.C.

Solo

Neanderthal

*

100,000 B.C.

*

*Neanderthal

Cro-Magnon

Neanderthal

Southern Ape

Australopithecus

750,000 B.C.

developed in Asia, the latter giving rise to groups that migrated into North and South America possibly as recently as 10,000 to 20,000 years ago. In our time, as we know (1492), representatives of the European faction migrated across the Atlantic, coming in contact with representatives of the "New World" faction in the Caribbean Sea region.

The descriptions of relationships given are of necessity somewhat vague due to limited information, and the migration picture as set forth may be somewhat oversimplified. Enough is known, however, to give substantiation to the general picture. A slight shift in pathways or dates would not change the general impressions appreciably. In time, it is likely that enough information will be obtained to enable confidence with respect to place or places of origin, and with respect to the lineage or the interbreeding mix that gave rise to the factions of modern man.

The distance from the Mediterranean area through the Bering Strait to Cape Horn at the tip of South America is about 15,000 miles, and from South Africa more than 20,000. These are phenomenal distances to have been traveled by meandering tribes motivated to move as their numbers increased and as the hunting areas had to be expanded. However, there was a period of 500,000 to 1 million years for it to happen and, as obvious, it did happen.

MAN'S SINGULAR POSITION AND THE "PLEISTOCENE OVERKILL"

Modern man as a species stands alone. He has no competitors in the use of tools, weapons, abstractions, language, logic, reason, and strategy planning. These newer capabilities combined with basic drives, assumed prerogatives, and adopted ethical standards, have made man a species very different from others. The extent to which these conditions appear to have made a difference is illustrated by a concept identified as the "Pleistocene Overkill."

Fossil records reveal that at different times during the long history of living things not only have new species come into being but, also, whole species have disappeared—become totally extinct. Of interest is the evidence showing that a large and seemingly disproportionate number of large animal types became extinct during the late Pleistocene Epoch.

Megafauna is a convenient term designating animals that weigh 50 kilograms or more (roughly 100 pounds). Analyses revealed that more than 50 whole genera—not species, but *genera*—disappeared during the late Pleistocene. This was several times greater than the losses detected for corresponding periods in earlier times. The differences have attracted the attention of investigators and studies of the situation have been made. A look was taken at smaller animal types and at plants to see if there were similar losses, but the findings were negative. The remains of plant life were examined to ascertain whether drought or some other condition may have reduced the food supply. Based on fossil records as revealed by pollen and other kinds of analyses, these findings were negative. Climate—average temperature, humidity, and rainfall—was also checked. Since the Pleistocene was a period of glaciation, there were noteworthy temperature and other changes during the interval, but these, like the other features mentioned, failed to correlate with the times of precipitous megafauna extinctions.

Figure 24 is a slightly simplified graph presented originally by Martin (*Nature*, **212**: 339, 1966). It calls attention to happenings in North America, Africa, and the Island of Madagascar, for which specific data are available. The drop in the respective curves indicates generic or species extinctions. The vertical dotted lines show when a worldwide climatic change occurred, mainly drought. This change did indeed coincide with the precipitous losses that occurred in North America, but not with those that occurred in the other locations. The only happening that Martin was able to find that correlated consistently throughout was human invasion. Martin has therefore raised serious question whether man with his fluted arrow points, his ability to use fire, his ability to cause stampedes of large animals over precipices, or to lure them into disadvantageous positions may not have contributed to or actually caused extinctions of certain forms of mastodons, elephants, rhinos, buffalos, horses, camels, and the like.

It is of course improbable that any single factor exerted sufficient influence to eliminate a well-established species, but it is entirely possible that a single factor could produce a final generalized fatal result. Whether the Martin hypothesis will hold true under continuing analysis and investigation remains to be

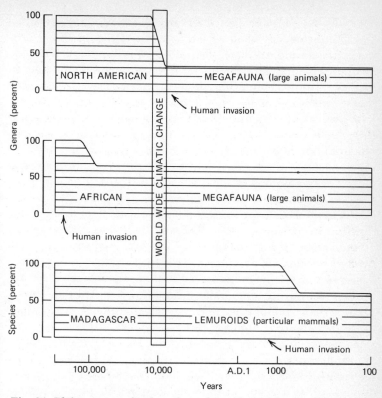

Fig. 24. Pleistocene extinction chronology (from Martin, *Nature*, 212: 399, 1966; with permission).

seen, but its claims are reasonable and its elements aid us in comprehending the molding influences responsible for man's present behavior.

By using tools, weapons, and strategies, early man had enormous advantage over other animal types. By maneuvering animals like mastodons into bogs or other unfavorable fighting areas, and by acting as organized hunting bands, man could overpower and kill creatures much larger than himself. Because of this ability and because of his ability to promote mass killings through the use of stampeding techniques, man undoubtedly squandered the booty of his kills. It was easy for primitive man to kill just to obtain hides needed for clothing or shelter, or particular bones needed as tools. This was quite unlike the killing done by fish, birds, and snakes where the entire prey is swallowed and the sole objective is to satisfy hunger.

It probably did not enter the minds of primitive men to ask about *rights* to live or about the lasting potential of resource reserves. Primitive man, like other creatures, lived by the *law of the jungle*—eat or be eaten. Primitive man obviously utilized his special advantages in the same way that a tiger uses his sharp teeth or an elephant his tusks or trunk. Further, it is obvious that primitive man, like other creatures, used a procedure with respect to food use that is as old as animal life itself. This was to use freely any food source that was available. Bees flit from flower to flower, going where the nectar is most readily available, and birds go from fruit to fruit where seeds and pulp are most plentiful. A few animals store food and some do so by means of fat reserves, but this is done pretty much in accord with what the involved individuals require for survival.

Man as a hunter, with his special hunting advantages and with his ways of utilizing products of the hunts, exhausted the sources of supply more rapidly. This necessitated continuous exploration and search for new hunting areas, and it accounts in part for man's tendency to move about over the face of the earth more than other species.

Man, with his special capabilities and tendencies, left his mark on the land. In Pleistocene time, this may well have contributed to, or even caused, the disappearance of whole genera of large animal types, but it did not *yet* constitute a threat to the process of life itself. However, should there have been a kind of omnipotent plot to do in the human species along with other species, and to divert substantially the cosmic process as it had been operating on planet earth, these directions of development could well have been a beginning.

Chapter 6

The Birth of Civilization

In Chapter 1, the earth was pictured as a culture tube inoculated with human beings—along with other organisms—which multiplied according to the compound interest law. Now we have just completed a characterization of the human species as essentially the only element in nature acting deliberately, if unwittingly, to augment the course of Nature.

It was during the Pleistocene that it all began. This is when a particular vertebrate species first walked upright and began development of an advanced intellect. Obviously, without the slightest awareness of what was happening, the human species began a course of action that multiplied its kind increasingly and in time carried its representatives to the ends of the earth, thus setting itself very much apart from all others. The Pleistocene, as has been indicated, began about 1 million years ago and it lasted until about 10,000 years ago. The Pleistocene was followed by an epoch identified by geologists as *Recent*. Thus far, the Recent Epoch represents a period only about one one-hundredth that of the Pleistocene. It is the period of modern man.

The legacy left by the Pleistocene, as far as species man was concerned, was articulate speech, a worldwide distribution of people, tribal life, elements of leadership, and a semblance of governance. Growing out of the expanding mental capability was the transconstitutive feature of curiosity—the desire to know, to know how—in order to harness and to utilize the forces and products of nature more effectively for man's own benefits, and without regard for conservation.

In a general way it can be said (see again Figure 1 of Chapter

1) that Nature, operating on planet earth, required about 1 billion years to produce life, 2 to 3 billion years additional to produce man, and only a few thousand more years to create the mind of man.

The purpose now is to understand and to go as far as possible in analyzing modern man's basic drives as they came into being, the occurrence of ethical codes and the way they have acted as determiners of behavior, and finally the formation of institutions and the occurrence of civilization. This we feel opens the way for dealing with the dilemma of expanding potential and tightening limitations.

LEVEL 6 THROUGH-PUT

In Chapter 3, five levels of through-put operation were described, starting with the simple reflex type of action and extending through operations with adaptive behavior. There is yet another level of systems operation and it is important in our discussion at this stage. This is through-put operation which occurs in groups of individuals the same as that which occurs in individuals. This kind of action we refer to as *societal through-put operation*—Level 6.

Figure 25 presents the concept. Societies as units also act as through-put information systems. Information as input comes into the system, the information is processed or evaluated in relation to needs of the system, and action as output is taken. In addition, a societal system is self-organizing and adaptive in

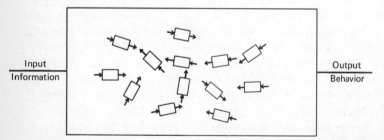

Fig. 25. Societal through-put system; community as an operative entity.

that the action taken is intended as favorable for the group. Societal systems are therefore purposive in the same way that individual organism systems are purposive. But, although there are similarities, there are also differences and these now need to be understood.

Organisms have brains or ganglia by means of which incoming information becomes integrated with basic drives and contained motivations—all existing as stored information. Where governments exist, societies also have a kind of brain that acts to set goals and to achieve motivation; very often, however, government as brain is remote and to a considerable extent apart from attitudes and public opinions as mass mind. Organisms have nerves and muscles as end organs in different parts of the body and through them out-going stimuli are transmitted efficiently and effectively in such a way as to obtain and maintain effective behavior in accordance with constantly changing situations. Society likewise has a reasonably good output communication system. By means of the public media of press, radio, and TV, and through law enforcement facilities, the people as constituent parts of the whole societal system or organism, are kept informed —but often on the basis of fixed and outmoded laws rather than moment-to-moment adaptive situations.

Organisms have highly efficient sense organs of a variety of types and an effective system of input nerves by which the headquarters integrative system is kept continuously informed—not only of conditions of the surrounding environment, but also of the welfare of constituent parts of the organism. The finger as a constituent part may, in effect, say "I hurt," thereby causing headquarters to direct the eyes to look; the eyes in turn then say, in effect, to headquarters "there is a foreign body," thus causing headquarters to direct the opposite hand to remove the irritating object. In democratic forms of government, the input function is of low order, and in authoritarian governments it is essentially absent. A vote every four years or a letter or phone call to the mayor or governor are not very effective ways of keeping the powers of government appraised on a moment-to-moment basis of the conditions of all the factions of society.

Some governments attempt to operate as democratic self-organizing adaptive systems (Level 6 through-put), but fall far short especially because of poor input. Poor input, in turn, prevents opportunity for feedback and thereby the opportunity for moment-to-moment integration of behavior. It is obvious that if organism behavior were to operate on the basis of fixed laws, which often are half measures because of compromise and are out-moded, the operative process would likewise be cumbersome, depressive, and debilitating. Level 6 of through-put operating at the level of government tends to be grossly inefficient.

GENERATION OF GOALS AND THE DYNAMICS OF INSIGHT

It has been emphasized in Chapter 3 that systems have little meaning except in terms of goals—the achievement of ends. Goals are targets. They are the object of action and they exert a molding or determining influence. Goals are important in individual behavior and they are important also in group behavior. Fundamental as goals are in societal functions, there is often a tendency to shy away from them, to avoid them, and to neglect them. The question here is how in self-organizing systems like organisms and societies, goals are generated and become determining influences—also, how goals can be kept commensurate with changing needs and opportunities.

There are at least three types of goals: (1) those set by the inherent design of systems, (2) those set by decree, and (3) those developed on a moment-to-moment or situation basis in accordance with needs and opportunities.

Examples of goals set by the design of systems are given as follows: (1) A radio is a device or system, which by electronic circuit design has music and news as its objective or goal. (2) A television set is a device or system, which by a different electronic design, has pictures as well as music and news as its objective. (3) Life as a process has survival as an objective and the biochemical processes involved are such that continuation is a feature; the flame of life burns as long as there is appropriate fuel. The goal in this case is inherent because of the nature of the process. (4) Evolution, as a process, has change combined with improvement in efficiency for survival as an inherent goal. (5) Natural selection, as part of the process of evolution, involves an inherent goal of improvement by continuous elimination of the less fit—be it a thing or process.

Examples of goals set by decree are choices or decisions resulting in laws, regulations, or directives that may be made on the basis of deliberations or simply by command.

Examples of goals developed on a moment-to-moment or situation basis are of the type involved in behavior where objectives must necessarily be different from moment-to-moment, depending on conditions. This kind of goal development occurs in connection with individual or group behavior where searching and adaptiveness are involved in relation to short-range or long-range situations.

Man has reacted oddly to goals. On the one hand he shies away from them—avoids talking about them; and, on the other, by the very act of doing, acts in agreement with them—goals that he may or may not have stopped to recognize. Much of what man does is in accordance with custom where goals are inherent but rarely thought about. Man, for example, participates in patriotic ceremonies and religious rituals very often without asking about goals or objectives. He acts in a particular way because others do. Goals set by Nature's design and the operation of natural laws, such as natural selection and survival of the fittest, are often held in awe and great respect by man. The setting of goals is regarded by many as beyond man, as the work of the Divine, making it a sacrilege should man be so presumptuous as to attempt to intervene. As pointed out, however, systems and systems operations make little sense except in terms of goals. Goals are important in mentative systems.

Development of goals has parallels with development of insights. Hutchinson (*Journal of Psychiatry*, 4:31, 1941) and Martin (*American Journal of Psychoanalysis*, 12:24, 1952) have both written perceptively about the dynamics of insight. They characterized the happenings leading to exclamations such as "eureka," "aha," "I've got it," "I have the answer"—the so-called "aha phenomenon." On the basis of work with psychiatric patients and of observations on "normal" people, it was pointed out that breakthroughs in comprehension and understanding usually occur unexpectedly—when having a shower, when walking to work, or when reading on another subject—but that such breakthroughs are preceded by two other phases. One is a substantial period of wallowing with the subject or problem, and the other is a period of relaxation or resignation. Problem resolution and the development of goals or insights are like doing jig-saw puzzles. One by one pieces keep dropping into place, but impasses may be reached. Parts of a problem become resolved, but somehow things simply do not progress. This may be the situation even after there has been a concentrated effort to achieve a resolution. The individual or the social group, as the case may be, may give up or simply suspend the problem for the time being. This is the second period. Then, out of the blue, and unexpectedly, a key piece is spotted or a key thought comes to mind, and everything falls into place. Teilhard de Chardin, in *The Phenomenon of Man* (p. 78) makes this wonderful comment: "In every domain, when anything exceeds a certain measurement, it suddenly changes its aspect, condition or nature. The curve doubles back, the surface contracts to a point, the solid disintegrates, the liquid boils, the germ cell divides, *intuition suddenly bursts upon the piled up facts.*" Insights are sudden perceptions of truth. Understandings and goals emerge from the interrelating of pieces of information—the associative function such as occurs in brains or computers. Goals and purpose arise from interacting information—from information dynamics. Goals may become fixed as in the case of laws, creeds, and dogmas, and they may be *symphonic*—changing from moment to moment, as required in adaptive behavior.

The strength and integrity of individuals or of social groups involves, in part, the ability to perceive the realities and the truths of Nature. Each step in the growth of awareness adds an increment of mentative competence.

MAN'S INHERENT DRIVES

Behind civilizations are the drives that impel individual human beings to behave as they do. (1) There is the drive to remain alive—a feature provided by the transconstitutive property of molecular replication. DNA as it operates in a cell or organism is both self-maintaining and self-organizing. (2) There is the drive or instinct to mate and reproduce by means of which the species is maintained. (3) There is the drive to learn. In sub-human organisms, the drive to search and explore is associated mainly, if not entirely, with acquisition of food and mating, but in human beings, it is associated with a compelling desire to know about Nature in as many aspects as possible. (4) There is the drive or instinct to defend territory—to possess or to own. Defense of property according to one's strength and special advantages goes far back in animal behavior. It is a primitive trait. (5) There is the instinct to acquire power—to utilize any advantage in gaining superiority or dominance over others. (6) In human beings, there is the instinct to be compassionate—to aid others in ways that are comforting and beneficial. The sixth drive or instinct, it will be noted, is essentially opposite in character to the others named, in that it implies concern for others as well as self—a feature important in the creation of civilizations. Various other drives could be mentioned, but these are sufficient for the purposes here.

ASSUMED PREROGATIVES

Stemming directly from primitive situations are certain assumed prerogatives that have been strong determiners of individual and group behavior and thereby of the direction of man's recent evolution. Freedom to help oneself to elements of the environment has been a mode of behavior since the beginning of animal existence. Bees in the field flit from flower to flower wherever the nectar is most plentiful. Similarly, birds or rodents in the wild partake of fruits and seeds without regard for the needs of others and also without regard for the need of seeds to produce another crop. Freedom to exploit the resources of nature with unconcern and abandon is deep-rooted and basically ingrained. It is *Nature acting in the raw*.

Another assumed prerogative is the right to kill—the right to kill in order that "I may eat the flesh of another and thus preserve the opportunity for my own survival;" the right to kill in self-defense in order that "I rather than the other creature can remain alive." This again is the law of the jungle. It also is deep-rooted and basically ingrained. In the jungle, it is the way an individual or species succeeds or fails, it is the way natural selection operates. Despite man's tendencies to be compassionate and to participate in civilized living, and almost irrespective of needs for food or materials, human beings also hold tenaciously to the right to kill and to make war on one's neighbors. Killing by means of war has been ritualized and institutionalized for the defense of honor, prestige, and ways of life.

A third assumed prerogative, which is deep-rooted and basically ingrained, is the right extending beyond the instinct to defend territory—to possess or to have ownership. Animals defend territory and so do human beings. Moreover, man-made laws provide sanction for the practice.

The last assumed prerogative to be mentioned is the right to acquire influence and power. In animals and human beings alike power accrues to him who holds advantages, be they physical prowess, intellect, or acquired wealth.

These are assumed prerogatives. They involve jungle behavior consisting of reckless abandon and rugged individualism. They are part of man's legacy from the past. In more recent times, the assumed objective to a very large degree has been *to get it now,* "to get it while you can," and by whatever means required—the oil, the minerals, indeed the treasures of the earth in general; think little of descendants and of future generations.

ETHICAL CODES AND PRINCIPLES

Man as a thinking, self-organizing, inventive, and creative creature has, in connection with group living, developed rules to live by—rules or general codes for conduct in dealing with problems and with others. Some of the more established of these, the same as in the case of drives and assumed prerogatives, arose out of the very nature of animal existence and, because of seeming naturalness and growing precedent, in time came to be strong governing elements of conduct and behavior.

In addition to governance influences stemming from the nature of existence itself, there were other types of influences, and questions have arisen as to whether certain of these were generated by the minds of men or by an intelligence beyond man. Consider the edict of Genesis which says "Be fruitful and multiply, fill the earth, subdue it and have dominion over it." Note the dictums "fill the earth," "subdue it," and "have dominion over it." At the same time, these are commands and stated privileges, and they are sanctioned by what is regarded by many as *Divine* utterance. Consider the *pioneer ethic of freedom*—freedom to search for new land, freedom to exploit the resources, and freedom to pollute at will, as well as freedom to grow and multiply. When there were unexplored land frontiers, freedom was the watchword and it was natural. Since in earlier times man's impact was small compared with that of nature, and since nature soon compensated for or obliterated the influences of man, there was no reason to be restrictive. Moreover, this kind of freedom, it can be said, had been ordained by the tradition of animalistic behavior existent since life began. Freedom to move about, to utilize with abandon, and to leave refuse without concern was part of the law of the wild.

Consider the *capitalistic ethic of more wealth and more influence and power*. This also has been ordained by animalistic tradition—that of the strongest taking the most. Furthermore, this ethic became extended in the *principle of excellence*. In education, the tendency is to reward the bright with scholarships, thereby discriminating against the not-so-bright. Likewise, in business, the tendency is to provide higher salaries for the more educated and more talented and even to permit the savings of the more fortunate to earn additionally by means of interest, all of which causes a widening gap between "haves" and "have-nots." Finally, for our purposes, consider what is sometimes identified as the *Judeo-Christian Ethic*, "By the sweat of thy brow, you shall earn a living." This dictum honors hard work and in effect says that "he who works earns a right to eat and thereby to live." In earlier times this principle was not only a practical matter, it was vital. Shirkers and idle hands brought hardship on entire groups. Thrift thus was rewarded and competition through free enterprise found its place—all of which fit well in the pioneer era. In the machine age, however, where a simple machine is able to do the work of 10, 100, or even 1000 men, the right to work and thus to earn a living and survive is thrown into considerable jeopardy—in principle, if not in reality. On the basis of the free enterprise approach, the tendency has been to say that "he who owns the machine is entitled to all of its earnings."

The ethical codes and principles mentioned center around the self-interest aspects of life, both with respect to individuals and groups. They also include elements of cooperation, which in human society have come to include ethical principles such as "turning the other cheek," "doing unto others as one would be done by," and "being my brother's keeper." Inherent in Nature's scheme since the beginning of animal life has been the element of self-interest and the assumption that one's own life takes precedence over all others. It is by this means that the surviving species endured. It included natural selection and it is the way evolution has taken place.

A hundred and eighty degrees around is *compassion*—a manifest desire to cooperate for the common good. Cooperation carries with it a principle precisely opposite to that of competition. Moreover, it carries with it a profound implication, namely that *selective coexistence is mutually beneficial*. In case of the human species, this includes selective coexistence not only of individuals and groups, but of other species as well. Honeybees, for example, are favored although mosquitos are discriminated against and eliminated; similarly, domestic animals and crops are bartered although mountain lions and weeds are exterminated. Implied again is the right and prerogative of destruction and exploitation as a means for survival. So great are man's manipulative skills in this regard at the present time, that whole species are being eliminated or built up according to man's will.

MYTHS

Man is an impatient creature. Not only does he have a curiosity and want to know, he will fabricate explanations. The many stories of *the creation*, the *virgin birth*, and of *life hereafter* are clear examples. Myths as such exist in reality and they exert a strong influence on human behavior. It is what people believe, more than what they know, that provides the greatest motivation for action.

SANCTION

One can ask how creeds and ethical codes, factual or mythological, came into being. Above we indicated that natural requirements make the basis and provide the sanction for certain kinds of conduct. Now we can go further. In some cases, rules of conduct are established directly by enactment of laws or regulations. Quite often, however, and particularly in earlier times, a more random procedure was employed—almost without awareness.

It is a part of man's makeup to have ambitions and aspirations. These may be in the form of desires to possess certain things or to achieve certain ends. When a thought, point of view, proposal, or practice appears not to conflict with individual or group interests, or simply is not noticed, it is tolerated. In time, then, precedent is established and that, in turn, establishes sanction. Custom and tradition tend then to take over, leading to rigid adherence almost irrespective of changing conditions and emerging conflicts. Custom and tradition are strong in their influence. They are not easily set aside or dislodged, in particular, when sustained by *Divine* sanction, by celebrity endorsement, by a feeling of loyalty, by patriotism, or the like.

INSTITUTIONALIZATION

One of the most prominent forces for the achievement of civilization has been the creation of institutions—the structuring of patterns of conduct or behavior, and of establishments. We speak of the institution of marriage, of the family, and of slavery; we also speak of the Smithsonian Institution or of the Ford Foundation as institutions. Institutionalization means shaping, designing, or molding for acceptability and use, be it a methodology, a procedure, or a type of conduct, on the one hand, or an organization with buildings, on the other. The creation of institutions was and is a means for accomplishing tasks that otherwise might remain unaccomplished or unaccomplishable; it is a way of assuring the attainment of goals and the preservation of selected practices, customs, and traditions.

When species man first operated in groups—hunting bands, let us say—certain leadership and organization was necessary in order to consolidate the effort and assure accomplishment of the tasks. Governance leading to government as a means of securing coordination and control was a natural response to needs and it was indeed a way of accomplishing tasks that otherwise could not have been accomplished. This has been and is a common pattern—organization in response to a need.

As indicated, institutions may come into being more or less automatically, simply by the people involved taking the most obvious course in response to problems. More often in present times, however, they are formed by means of founding documents or charters, which set forth goals and objectives, and may even lay down precise procedures. In both cases, the purpose is to meet a group need or to serve the public interest in some way. Successful institutions achieve their purposes, especially in earlier years, but very often undergo natural but unanticipated changes that have a stultifying influence on community cultural advancement.

The need may be for a school, a college, a hospital, a fire department, a police force, a labor union, or a fraternal order. It might even be for a system of economy such as the Common Market of Western Europe. A school, a hospital, or a police department may be formed, and for a period they may serve the public interest effectively as intended. But, in time they grow. Many people become dependent on the existence of the institution itself, causing their concern to transfer from the welfare of the community, which the institution was intended to serve, to the welfare of the institution itself. With time, the teachers, the nurses, the doctors, the firemen or the police, in self-interest, strike against the public, demanding greater income or other benefits, and thus alienating the group that brought them into existence. The institutional people thus promote their own self-interests as the matter of primary concern rather than the welfare of the public they were expected originally to serve. There is thus a displacement of goals and authority, and organization "dry rot" sets in.

Consider the labor union that has successfully insured the rights of workers but is then faced with going out of business or developing new goals. Consider the fund raising organizations that give support to the development of a vaccine for the cure of a disease, and then a vaccine is discovered. Again, it is a matter of going out of business or of keeping the cause alive in some way simply because it makes a profitable basis for fund raising. Very often the second course of action is taken, making the institution itself the object to be served rather than the community it was formed to serve. Organizations in time institutionalize, becoming entities with their own rights and prerogatives. It is easy to see that as second-, third-, and fourth-order institutionalization occurs, the overall societal condition grows weaker with spreading degradation and discontent.

Consider the institutions of government. Governments are formed to serve the people—that is, apart from those authoritarian ones, which are formed to rule the people. Even democratic governments usurp power very fast—in fact, it is usually assumed from the beginning that anyone who strongly opposes the form or design of government is automatically a traitor and a subject to be shot forthwith. Governments, being in the position to tax, rapidly assume the role of public benefactor, determining who shall get the schools, the roads, the welfare, the subsidies, the public assistance, the grants for research, the charters for exploration, the contracts for updating weapons systems, and the like. Governments have a way of building institutional and personal power, even in democratic countries. They serve the people, but in ways that cause the government and government positions to become stronger. The emphasis is on how the government, with all its political jockeying, can somehow perform the jobs rather than how the jobs can be done more efficiently by the people themselves.

The yielding of power by the people and organization dry-rot are the prices paid for the use of many methodologies now being employed. Societal operation, as we now know it, is of low order from the standpoint of effectiveness or efficiency, and the reasons are fairly obvious. We operate societal systems and institutions on a static instead of a dynamic base. Societal operation, as we promote it, is governed almost entirely by fixed provisions—charters, laws, regulations, precedents, and traditions. Consider the behavior of organisms—of a human being—if his behavior were governed by experiences of the past rather than situations of the moment. The behavior of organisms is so coordinated, meaningful and efficient simply because the organismic system is both sensitive to and responsive to its environment on a continuously changing basis. Behavior in a fully adaptive system is like orchestration. It is *symphonic*, continually changing with its crescendos and pianissimos set to a changing mood. Because of the way we operate our societal systems, they are only partially adaptive at best. They are like brain-injured children where there is faulty communication and control—where there is poor orchestration. In the mentally retarded or in societies, the behavior may be unresponsive and lethargic, it may be hyperactive, it may involve stammering and stuttering.

Civilization has remained alive and made progress because the forces of organization have been greater than the forces for disorganization, but the margin of difference varies and it could disappear altogether.

Chapter 7

Explosive Effects of Information Generativeness

The task set is that of comprehending human progress more completely in individuals and great groups of individuals. Two central points have been made. One is that advanced intellect, as we know it, occurred on planet earth in species man very late in evolutionary history; the other is that information interacting with information is generative. These two facts of nature provide a departure point for further consideration.

By standing apart and looking in perspective, as well as we can, at human intellect and information generativeness, we sense and can see a special situation building—one of accelerating change leading inevitably to some kind of fracture point. Generativeness means amplification. If, then, information is accumulating at an ever-faster rate, we are compelled to expect that an explosive situation of some kind is in the making—and one for which we have little or no precedent for use as an aid in evaluating or in managing. Somehow one senses that a transconstitutive mass mind transformation is occurring and that man's present dilemmas are associated with this pervasive and generally ominous change. As a step in characterizing the developments, let us set forth additional background.

THE SCIENTIFIC METHOD AND ITS TRANSCONSTITUTIVE IMPACT

Man inherited from animal ancestors a curiosity—a compulsion to explore. True, it was no more than a compulsion to explore for food, shelter, and mates, but this was a beginning. Extension to include search for materials needed for tools and weapons was a comparatively small step, but the extension to include exploration for the sake of knowing—it would seem—must be classed as a major change.

Early man had a compulsion or passion to know—one so strong that if satisfying answers were not immediately available, the tendency not only was to speculate but also to fabricate. This, as already pointed out, gave rise to mythology, ritual and religious worship, all of which has exerted a strong influence on man's behavior—actually until quite recent times and to some extent including the present time. Philosophers and theologians, both before and after the time of Christ, became expert in the art of reasoning and deduction. Greek logicians and mathematicians provided a strong leadership and did much by precise rationalization to bring forth the axioms of mathematics which, among other things, gave rise to the laws of motion and enabled prediction of the movement of heavenly bodies. This in general was pretty much the situation up to the time of Galileo (1545–1642).

In the words of Asimov (*The New Intelligent Man's Guide to Science*, 1965), "The Greeks, by and large, had been satisfied to accept the 'obvious' facts of nature as starting points for their reasoning. It is not on record that Aristotle ever dropped two stones of different weight to test his assumption that the speed of fall was proportional to an object's weight. To the Greeks, experimentation seemed irrelevant. It interfered with and detracted from the beauty of pure deduction. Besides, if an experiment disagreed with a deduction, could one be certain that the experiment was correct? Was it possible that the imperfect world of reality would agree completely with the perfect world of abstract ideas, and, if it did not, ought one to adjust the perfect to the demands of the imperfect? To test a perfect theory with imperfect instruments did not impress the Greek philosophers as a valid way to gain knowledge."

Galileo approached the questions of Nature differently. He performed tests. Among other things, it is said that he dropped a ten-pound and a one-pound sphere simultaneously from the Leaning Tower of Pisa. The thump of the two balls on the ground in the same split second, as Asimov points out, "killed Aristotelian physics." Galileo's contribution consisted of elevating induction above deduction as the logical method of science. Instead of building conclusions on an assumed set of generalizations, the inductive method starts with observations and derives generalizations. Whereas Greek philosophers of the fifteenth century minimized the role played by induction, there were those in addition to Galileo who were beginning to look on induction as the essential process of gaining knowledge and the only way to justify generalizations. In England, beginning about 1645, a group interested in newer scientific approaches was formed. At first it was called the Royal Society of London for Improving Natural Knowledge, and later simply the Royal Society.

The emerging point of view was opposite to that of Greek philosophers and earlier scholars. Instead of considering the real world an imperfect representation of truth, the tendency was to consider generalizations imperfect representations of the real world. As Asimov has stressed, no amount of inductive testing can render a generalization completely and absolutely valid. Even though vast numbers of observations tend to bear out a generalization, a single observation that contradicts or is inconsistent with it must force its modification. Increasingly, there emerged a precept or article of faith. It was that *the facts of Nature are verifiable*. It was an acceptance of the idea, as Asimov has stated, that *Nature plays fair*.

The conclusion that Nature plays fair and that the facts of Nature are verifiable was new. It constituted a shift from conjecture and isolated imaginative thinking to thinking involving hypothesis backed by experimental testing. Acceptance of this idea, as we know, became the foundation of modern natural philosophy and the basis of modern science, involving observation, classification, quantification, measurement, calculation, comparison, evaluation, and the like. This simple shift in a single point of view was a major one. It marked a turning point in human history and in the direction of earth cosmology, for it laid the groundwork for technology and the industrial revolution.

SECRECY

Along with acceptance of the idea that Nature plays fair came another innovative change—one that seems commonplace now, but one that made a great deal of difference only a comparatively short time ago. This was free and cooperative communication between all scientists. History reveals that the Pythagoreans of ancient Greece were a secret society and kept their mathematical discoveries to themselves; also that the alchemists of the Middle Ages deliberately obscured their writings to restrict the availability of their results, such as they were, to as small a group as possible. The first moves to publish openly were considered a betrayal and a disregard of the privileges that should accrue to those who discover.

From information dynamics, we now know that it is information in motion that amplifies—not that which is stored and is thereby static. Free dissemination of hypotheses and the results of experimental investigations to test them brought forth an avalanche of information and discoveries that has not commenced to slow down even yet.

INFORMATION EXPLOSION

The stage was set. By the end of the eighteenth century much classification of the things of nature had been completed—especially the minerals and living things—and people were busy analyzing, discovering, and inventing. Water and steam power began to replace manpower and horsepower. Machines and factories came into being. Reliance on the idea that Nature plays fair was valuable. It was worth money. Industry had its birth.

Silently and almost unnoticed information accumulated. Libraries and museums were established. Maps, formulas, demonstration materials, and many kinds of technical information were available for all to see and experience. There was indeed opportunity for information to interact with information.

It is reported that in recent decades, the amount of technical information available doubles every ten years. Further, there are at present close to 100,000 scientific and technical journals being published throughout the world and that the number of these is doubling every 15 years. This means that every 10 years or so the amount of information is twice that accumulated in all time previously. It means also that the increase is exponential with time and therefore getting faster and moving toward some kind of turning point. Even if the estimates of increase rates are in error as much as 100 percent, which is unlikely, the situation is explosive, leading either to a substantial slowdown or to some catastrophic change.

As late as 100 years ago, it was possible for an educated man to have a reasonable comprehension of the whole of scientific and technical knowledge. This, of course, has changed markedly. To aid in comprehending knowledge more adequately, abstract journals were created and, in time, their numbers came to increase exponentially. In turn, analytical computers have come to be used to abstract the abstract journals and the increase in analytical computers is now exponential. At this point, question begins to arise concerning man's relationship to accumulating knowledge.

PROMOTION OF RESEARCH

During the past several decades, and especially since World War II, *research and development* has been a watchword expression. Government and foundation support of research also skyrocketed with doubling every few years. Justification for the support of research during the 1940s and 1950s was mainly the prospects for improvement in health, productivity, and defense. In a matter of years, these goals were achieved to a surprising degree. Most infectious diseases were brought under control; production went to overproduction or overproduction potential, in many areas; and armaments went to overkill on a global basis. Achievement of research goals, however, seemed to make little difference in the attitudes about support of research. In recent years, a prevailing view has been that research is good—an end in itself and a way of life that enhances the dignity of man. There has been a tendency to justify research by saying that *if a thing can be done, it should be done.*

During the period of the 1960s, it became apparent in the United States that if federal support of research were to continue to increase at existing rates, soon the entire gross national product would be consumed for this purpose alone. A slowdown was thus inevitable, and already there has been a cut in the rate of spending for research. The recent happenings and the trends of events in this area of human expression, however, provide a basis for searching questions.

Suppose funding were not a limiting factor. How much research would we as a people choose to support? Would it be twice as much, 10 times as much, or 100 times as much? Is research and exploration really a good way of life and suitable for still more people? Would it prove satisfying to a substantial proportion of the people? If there were no limiting factors, how fast would we like the accumulation of information to be? How much new information can the average individual cope with each day or each year? How much new information can a society cope with or how much should it store, in a year or a generation?

We have been alluding to scientific and technical information, but the same questions apply when views and facts about religious, cultural, and aesthetic values are included as information.

UNPREDICTABILITY AND INEXORABLENESS OF INFORMATION GENERATIVENESS

What the transconstitutive consequence of information interacting with information will be is not forseeable, nor is the application of information predictable. When Gregor Mendel, shortly before 1900, studied heredity in the garden pea, he scarcely could have anticipated that the principles he set forth would become the basis of vast livestock and crop improvement throughout the world—not to mention eugenic measures. When Einstein in 1905 set forth the mass-energy formula as a means of explaining the operation of Nature, he probably did not anticipate the decisive weaponry that would emerge directly from his formula. When Henry Ford in his workshop invented the combustion motor, he could hardly have foreseen the magnitude of the great industry that was to arise from his ideas. Information interacting with information, we repeat, is generative. Moreover, when there is opportunity for information associativeness (as can happen in brains, computers, and societies), generativeness seems destined to occur.

There is thus a kind of inexorableness about the amplification of information. Man, because of his curiosity as a basic drive, searches for information; because of his brain, he stores and associates it; and because information interacting with information in his brain or in the public mind is generative, new information is created. All of this is occurring because of man's emergence as a creature of intellect. Unless man is somehow "turned off" as man, increasing information generativeness is to be anticipated. Actually, because of computer potential, such generativeness may occur irrespective of species man. This remarkable thought will be explained in the next section.

MENTATIVE FUNCTION TRANSCENDING
HUMAN BEINGS

Already it has been emphasized that the information available, even in specialized fields, is now often beyond the comprehension of individual human minds. As recent as 100 years ago, the head of a business, an industrial plant, a factory, an army, a research laboratory, or a government, or the leader of a research field, could pretty well be abreast of what was going on and give carefully considered guidance to the activities over which he had supervision. Now the situation is different. Increasingly, there is reliance on intelligence reports, committee evaluations, and computer abstracts, if even a fraction of understanding is to be had about the rapidly changing conditions and states of affairs. All too often these days executives sit in high-paneled offices and flash out directives based on *seat-of-the-pants hunches* more than on concrete information and genuine sensitivity—not because facts and information are not available but, instead, because of the overpowering task of comprehending it. A consequence not too infrequently is that one executive remains until he makes a serious mistake, at which time he is replaced and the cycle starts over again. More successful executives of large organizations rely increasingly on machines, acting to program in a new principle or to introduce a policy change now and then as needed, but otherwise letting the system operate adaptively, like an organism with sensors, processors, and expressors.

Processors, as computers, are in certain respects more efficient than human beings. They can store infinitely more information and they can process it in certain ways much more effectively and rapidly. A whole medical or legal education can be programmed into a computer in a matter of hours. Then, given a set of symptoms, or the facts bearing on a case, the machine can diagnose fully as reliably as physicians or lawyers—and probably much more so. Naturally enough, executives, professional men, legislators, and others are reluctant to relinquish their prerogatives, but increasingly they are being forced to do so. A kind of hiatus is being created inasmuch as the minds that created machine intelligence are, in some measure, being displaced by it. It seems that man, in seeking the assistance he needs, is being set aside as a key governance entity in Nature's cosmic process simply by the inexorable forces inherent in the system.

It would appear, in fact, that Nature, in evolving intellect and an animalistic approach to problem resolution, has created rather suddenly a kind of juggernaut—one that will have disruptive if not catastrophic effects unless wisely managed by man himself.

Chapter 8

Societal Systems and the Affluent Life

Man in his development has struggled continuously for an easier and better way of life—one involving less work for sustaining the body and more time for exploration and leisure. A type of existence involving something less than full time required for making a living, comparative freedom from drudgery and including some amount of wealth, is identified as the *affluent life*.

During the period of Pioneer America, achievement of an affluent life was anticipated and alluded to as the *American Dream*. At that time, achievement of the American Dream was clearly a matter of conquering the forests, harnessing the streams, and utilizing the mineral resources. In time, the American Dream was achieved in considerable measure but, as we now know, this did not free man of problems. In the analysis being made, it is important to sense and appreciate still more completely the motivation and the forces that acted to catapult mankind into the present state of complexity and bewilderment.

INDUSTRIALIZATION

Early man, as we have recognized, was a hunter and operated in hunting bands. With increasing capability and know-how, this way of gaining a livelihood was extended to fishing, the raising of crops, and the domestication of animals.

Agriculture, as a way of life, proved successful in many parts of the world. On farms, people lived close to the soil and, to a large degree, in harmony with it. Products were taken from the soil, and to a considerable extent returned to it. In time, mills and factories were built, causing manufacturing in itself to become profitable and a way of life. With the right of individuals to own property, with the privilege of buying and selling, and with the opportunity to issue and purchase stocks, the industrial society came into being. Large corporations were formed, gigantic enterprises could be and were carried out, and people derived great wealth from their investments.

During the first half of the twentieth century—that is, from 1900 to 1950—manufacturing had become so successful in Western Europe and North America that leaders in most countries of the world sought industrialization as the best means to economic improvement and a better way of life. Nowhere was this attitude and commitment better revealed than at the First Geneva Conference on Peaceful Uses of Atomic Energy in 1954. The view and the hope then was that even the countries without coal, petroleum, or water power could utilize nuclear energy and thereby industrialize. Representatives from almost every country in the world presented papers indicating interest and varying degrees of progress in this direction. The attitude has continued even to the present time, although in some places, doubt is beginning to creep in concerning industrialization as a panacea.

CHAMBER OF COMMERCE MERRY-GO-ROUND

Economic development, as visualized by many, occurs in terms of growth—growth in population, growth in industrial productivity, and growth in resources utilization. It is a kind of merry-go-round and the Chamber of Commerce justifying argument is often that: population is needed to take advantage of the business opportunities, and then that more business is needed to provide jobs and income for the growing population. The action is much like that of the *Ouroboros* worm swallowing his tail. The idea of growth as the main pathway to a better life is deeply embedded in the minds of more advanced people and it is strong even today.

DEMOGRAPHIC TRANSITION

Demographers, as statistical analysts, have studied population growth in relation to economic development and have devised the concept of the *demographic transition*. This is a model of human societal function showing how population behavior tends to vary with economic development.

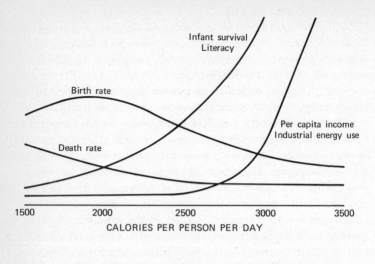

(Representative of level–of–living of economic development)

Fig. 26. Graph showing the relationship of birth rates, death rates, infant survival, literacy, per capita income, and industrial energy use, to caloric intake per person per day as representative of economic development. Progression by a population from left to right on this kind of scale is *demographic transition.*

The generalized picture is given in Figure 26, based on data obtained from *United Nations Demographic and Statistical Year Books* pertaining mainly to the period 1950 to 1955. Importantly, data are available for most of the countries of the world showing birth and death rates, per capita food consumption per day, literacy rates, infant mortality, per capita income, and per capita energy consumption, as well as many other features.

In Figure 26, caloric intake per person per day was used as the basis for comparison because caloric intake—level of feeding—is easy to understand and at the same time is representative of the level of living or economic development. The point being made is stronger when protein intake is used instead of total caloric intake, but protein data for the period considered are not as complete. The graph starts at the left with feeding at the level of 1500 calories per person per day, which is the level of bare subsistence. At the opposite end, the figure is 3500, which is not gluttony but bordering on it.

Note that with increasing caloric intake per person per day, birth rates tend at first to rise and then to fall away, whereas death rates drop away continuously. To interpret the curves a bit, it appears that as the feeding level changes from 1500 to 2000 calories, the general health improves, making the reproductive capability greater, with further improvement in nutrition, other activities are enabled by increasing affluence, which then compete with childbearing and bring it down. Death rates, on the other hand, show a continuous decrease with improvement in nutrition. The demographic transition, therefore, is defined as *increasing birth rates and falling death rates followed by a decline in birth rates and a continuing fall in death rates.*

With increasing affluence as represented by caloric intake, notice also what happens with respect to literacy rates, infant survival (the opposite of infant mortality), per capita income (per year) and industrial energy use (in terms of tons of coal equivalent per person per year)—the latter being representative of the level of industrialization. Since the curves for these features turn upward with increase in caloric intake instead of remaining parallel with the caloric intake line, it means that these elements increase even more rapidly. The curve for infant survival and literacy follows a smooth course indicating a direct relationship to nutrition or other elements of affluence associated with it. On the other hand, the curve for per capita income and use of industrial energy make a sharp upward turn when the caloric intake is about 3000 calories per person per day. Thus, when people are able to feed at the level of 3000 calories per day, the level of affluence is usually such that at least some of the income can go into savings and investment, making the earnings even greater, and enabling greater use of power equipment, including dish washers, automobiles, and bulldozers.

Figure 26 is a generalized picture of what happens with advancement in economic improvement. It is a kind of model useful in analyzing and understanding societal operation and behavior, and it is useful as a basis for making estimates of costs involved in moving factions or countries of people forward on the scale of economic development. It implies that quality of life in terms of health and creature comforts tends to coincide with economic improvement. There have been exceptions to this kind of societal behavior, of course, but it happens frequently enough that demographers and analysts of various types offer it as a useful and important guide.

The demographic transition, as a model, has comprised the basis for much optimism about industrialization. It is argued that along with industrialization, economic improvement occurs, and that along with economic improvement, birth and death rates drop and standards and levels of living increase dramatically. For political leaders, public planners, and promoters, this is a very attractive picture. Industrialization, by whatever means, appeals to many as the one best means of achieving the affluent life—of achieving the American Dream on a world basis and of enabling people everywhere to get over into the *Land of Milk and Honey*. Of fundamental importance, however, is the fact that countries and factions of people can and do move backward as well as forward on the scale of economic development and, in order to understand the direction of movement, it is necessary to know something about the factors that govern the movement.

ECONOMIC DETERMINERS

In dealing with economic development, there are negative as well as positive forces that must be taken into account. Industrial energy is a positive force, and if its per capita use is increasing, the economic condition can be said to be improving. On the other hand, if per capita use is decreasing, the economic condition must be said to be deteriorating. There is thus a kind of supply and demand situation with population growth acting as a negative force to counteract economic improvement. Standards and levels of living vary with the number of people making demands for products, on one side, and with the creation of products (or wealth) on the other. They vary also with the amount of productive land, with the bountifulness of natural resources, with the inventiveness and industriousness of the people, with the accumulated technical know-how and with the status of health—among other things. When each of these is weighed and measured in a meaningful manner, and the quantities are put into a well-designed formulation, a *situation index* figure is obtained, one representative of standards and levels of living in much the same way that the Dow-Jones Industrial Average is representative of stock market behavior. Obtaining such a figure at different times for a faction or nation of people shows how they may be changing on the scale of economic development; obtaining it for different factions or groups enables comparisons of achievement in these respects.

Here we should recognize that quality of life consists of more than the heatlh and creature comforts governed or enabled by economic development. However, inasmuch as the so-called finer things of life—virtue, integrity, and respect—tend in some measure to correlate with standards and levels of living, the multiple factor analysis or situation index approach can be used with some confidence as a method of evaluation for quality of life as well as for standards and levels of living.

Without going into measurements and calculations, it is easily apparent that a central determiner of standards and levels of living, including quality of life, is number of people making demands—that is, population, more particularly, population growth rates. Likewise, it is apparent that a key limiting factor is land area, including natural resources. In the overall equation, these elements—population and land resources—act against each other and, because of their central significance, to a large degree determine standards and levels of living or economic development.

Societies, as stressed, function as systems. They have an input of information and materials and there is an output of behavior. The degree of consistency of ouput with respect to input depends on the efficiency of communication and control within the system. Societies are often inefficient because of several factors: (1) inability to formulate standards and goals; (2) inability to formulate realistic policy once goals are set; and (3) inability to translate policy into action. These are mainly problems of communication and control. The weak determiners can be identified and evaluated. Moreover, overcoming them is a definite possibility.

In the unfolding picture, we need next to develop impressions of population growth behavior in relation to the sustaining power of the earth.

PROCREATION

Reproduction is a strange phenomenon. In higher forms, including man, it is bisexual. It involves two human beings, a female and a male, to initiate a new human life, the first to provide the ovum and the second to provide the fertilizing sperm. Two forces or processes in Nature act to insure that fertilization occurs: one is the parental instinct, the desire to have offspring, and the other is the sexual instinct, the desire to satisfy sexual passions, which result in sexual union and the deposit of sperm for fertilization. Population growth, in its natural form, has been, and still is, determined largely by these two elements, particularly sexual passions.

With respect to the perpetuation of life, Nature is bounteous. Each human female in her reproductive lifetime—from 15 to 45 years of age, producing one ovum each menstrual cycle—is capable of generating well over 300 ova. Likewise, each human male producing 200 to 500 million sperm per ejaculate—which may be as often as one to several times a week—generates almost countless numbers of germ cells in a lifetime. Yet, as we know, it is rare that more than eight or ten male and female germ cells will be used per couple for actual reproduction in a lifetime.

With respect to the reproductive process and how it builds population, there is a unique feature in the human species that deserves mention here. In subhuman mammalian forms (and many others, as well), reproduction is confined to specific seasons of the year, and receptivity of the female is limited to the period of heat that is associated with the moment of ovulation in the estrous cycle. In human beings, sexual activity and conception take place at all seasons of the year, and the human female is sexually receptive throughout the estrous cycle irrespective of the time of ovulation. Nature, through evolutionary changes, has acted to cause sexual activity in the human species to serve a purpose well beyond that of reproduction alone. Moreover, as will be indicated next, human management is aiding this trend even more.

By means of contraception in its many forms, together with various abortion techniques, sex is being retained for its own emotional and other values. This in itself is a transconstitutive step of significance, but it introduces another, which may be fully as noteworthy, or more so. It makes reproduction subject almost exclusively to the human will rather than sexual passions. This situation is new in Nature's scheme and it raises important questions concerning the virtues of freer sex and concerning ability of the human species to maintain itself if procreation is made completely subject to the human will. The question is whether the parental instinct, apart from the sexual instinct, is sufficiently strong to cause the race or species to maintain itself. Whatever the outcome, man as well as nature must accept the credit.

With this amount of information about factors acting to affect reproduction, we shall consider how populations have grown, are growing and how different elements are acting to augment growth rates.

POPULATION GROWTH

How population increase has occurred in the world has been stated impressively by Philip Hauser (*The Population Dilemma*, 1969): "It . . . took all the millennia before 1650 that man had been on this globe to reach a total of half a billion persons. But to add a second half billion took only two centuries (before 1850); a third half billion less than half a century (before 1900); a fourth half billion little more than a quarter of a century

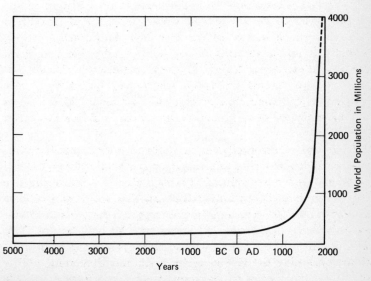

Fig. 27. World population growth.

(shortly before 1925); a fifth half billion less than a quarter of a century (by 1950). The sixth half billion added to world population required only ten years (by 1960), and the seventh addition of half a billion took only eight years (by 1968)." As Hauser states, "These numbers demonstrate dramatically why the accelerated rate of population growth has been called the 'population explosion'."

The recent explosive character of population growth is revealed a second way by Table 3, and a third way by Figure 27.

Table 3. Historical Events and World Population Growth Rates

Date	Methods and Means of Earning a Livelihood	Percent Population Increase per Year
5500–3000 B.C.	Food gathering Hunting Development of Language	0.04
3000–850 B.C.	Building towns Tilling the soil Invention of writing Discovery of metals	0.06
850 B.C.–A.D. 1650	Intensive agriculture Manufacturing Trade	0.07
1650–1750	Colonization Industrialization	0.29
1750–1800	Continuation of colonization Continuation of industrialization	0.44
1800–1850	Improved travel Communications	0.51
1850–1900	Health improvements Increased technology	0.63
1900–1950	Electronics development Discovery of atomic energy	0.75
1950–1970	Computer technology Space exploration	1.20
1967*		1.9

SOURCE: Adapted in part from Huxley, *Harper's Magazine,* 1950.
   * United Nations 1967 *Demographic Yearbook.*

As indicated in Table 2, the world population increase rate in 1967 was calculated to be 1.9 percent. This means that with a continuation of the 1.9 increase rate, the population of the world would double in approximately 35 years. For comparison, increase rates of representative parts of the world are given as follows:

North America	1.3
South America	1.7
Europe	0.8
Asia	1.5
Central America	3.5
Ireland	0.4
United Kingdom	0.6
United States	1.3
China	1.4
India	2.4

Figures indicate that population increase rates are lower in European countries and that they are higher—in some cases substantially higher—in other parts of the world. Calculations reveal that with continuation of present-world population increase rates for 600 years—comparatively a very short period in human history—there would be one person for each square foot of land area of the earth. When one travels across the world by automobile or airplane and sees vast unoccupied areas, this fact is difficult to appreciate or accept. It is only when careful statistical projections are made that the full impact comes through.

EARTH'S SUSTAINING POWER

Various analysts have considered the dimensions of the earth and the extent of its resources, and have then calculated the earth's carrying capacity in terms of human beings. Assumptions, of course, were necessary with respect to food intake levels, crop productivity, man's inventiveness in synthesizing food and other products, degrees of industrialization, tolerable levels of environmental contamination, and the like. Inasmuch as man's inventiveness is not easy to predict, the evaluations have limited significance at best, but nevertheless provide meaningful ball park figures.

Estimates of the earth's population carrying capacity have varied from 10 to 50 billion, depending on the standards and levels of living that would be acceptable and tolerable. Statistical data reveal that when the concentration of people in a country or territory exceeds one person per acre of usable land, the quality of life tends to deteriorate.

The total land area of the earth is approximately 35.7 billion acres, and about half of this is at present unusable due to severe cold and excessive dryness. More than this, increasing amounts of choice land are being taken out of production each year and devoted to locations for roads, cities, urban communities, airports, and public facilities of every kind. Even apart from availability of food and water, and from environmental pollution, to support 50 billion people would require giving up most of our parks and national forests; it would mean giving up most of our outdoor playgrounds, golf courses, and recreational areas; it would mean hydroponic and feed-lot agriculture primarily; it would mean farming the mountain sides as well as the hills and valleys; and, increasingly, it would mean life in skyscrapers, on floating islands, and under the seas.

The earth's human population is now about 3.5 billion; it is doubling about every 35 years and the doubling time is decreasing, as we have seen. This means that with continuation of the present growth pattern—that is, without growth rates any higher than at present—the 10 billion population level would be exceeded in about 60 years and the 50 billion level in a little less than 150 years. Even assuming that life could be tolerated when the population is 15 to 20 times what it is at present (50 billion divided by present level of 3 billion), and that man's ingenuity would somehow make the deserts and iced-in areas productive and inhabitable, this would accommodate only three to four more population doublings. In other words, such remarkable and seemingly impossible accomplishment would cover the needs of only an additional 100 to 150 years, leaving no tangible prospects for growth beyond another century or so.

INEXORABLENESS

Estimates of the sort just made make certain points abundantly clear.

1. They show that the compound interest law has inundative and explosive potential when numbers are large.

2. They make evident a major change that is happening with respect to population growth rate behavior—either voluntary on the part of man or forced by Nature.

3. They obviate the necessity of intelligent management if precipitous societal degradation on a world basis is to be avoided.

4. They predict that human life 50 to 100 years from now will be drastically different, either as a result of extensive reform or extensive deterioration.

Whether there can be half-way or intermediate measures will be matters for later consideration.

Chapter 9

Inevitability of Drastic Change

At the outset of this treatise, it was stated that the human species by its action and its behavior is on collision course with the conditions of Nature, and that precipitous degradative change is not only in the making but will intensify unless unprecedented alterations in behavior and direction of movement are made almost at once. Throughout this text, the human species has been characterized as one whose destiny is being determined increasingly by its own mental and functional development, but in accordance with principles and practices that are primitive, discordant with Nature, and threatening to continued species existence. The objectives here are to look still more closely at the discordant tendencies and to deal with the question of whether any course other than drastic change is likely or possible.

THE GENERALIZED PATTERN

In Nature's system, there are forces for organization and forces for disorganization, as we have seen. As we have also discussed, it is the difference between the level of disorganization and the level of organization that provides a margin for life, a margin for intellect, and a margin for societal behavior. Life and intellect acting together, it is apparent, constitute and involve a process of achieving organization that in turn acts to aid survival and performance, leading thus to societal operation.

In general, Nature operates at random, chancing on molecular configurations, informational combinations, and societal precepts that in some instances have provided positive and in others negative potential for life and intellect. Previous to the intelligence of man, survival of a process, a species, or a concept depended almost altogether on natural selection and survival of the fittest, thus involving change but not a specified direction or any preferential favoring of any species or thing. Man, because of his ability first to comprehend and then to augment Nature's random operation, has acquired a particularly advantageous position in the living world. In accordance with his instincts and traditions, he has sought to direct Nature's action not only to favor survival of his species, but also to make the conditions of his existence more "enjoyable" and more "satisfying" from the standpoint of his own goals, aspirations, and general well-being. Of importance to our thesis is recognition that the highly significant role of directing Nature was assumed by man casually, almost automatically, and almost without awareness that it was being done. Moreover, it was assumed with little or no more concern about trends and consequences than was shown by less comprehending species as they performed the tasks required for survival. Let us recognize this unconcerned, although highly significant method of dealing with Nature's processes as the *laissez faire* or simply the seat-of-the-pants approach to life already mentioned.

Inherent in the overall cosmologic process as it operates on planet earth and as it involves the human species, have been the natural limitations, the instinctive drives of man, man's assumed prerogatives, his moral values, his emerging ethical codes, his tendency to amplify his powers through discovery, invention, and industrialization, and the societal goals—mythological and realistic. Within the confines of this mix of influences, man has developed a behavior and forged a way of life, with results and consequences that have had a negative as well as a positive effect regarding organization as it benefits man's species, but with a margin thus far on the positive side. In the past, man's mistakes in judgment, his insensitivity to conditions, and his ineptness in dealing with situations, have been catastrophic on occasions, but never until the present period have they affected so completely the entire species on a global basis and been so much a threat to species existence. In history, whole civilizations have arisen and disappeared, but because of lack of contact with other civilizations such occurrences tended to be isolated events. Now a disease outbreak, a stock market slump, a shift in gold standard, discovery of a scientific principle, or the eruption of hostilities anywhere in the world can, and has in recent years, affected the whole of mankind. Because of the present worldwide system of communication and transportation, the human species is acting as a whole although society is only organized to operate as factions or nations—a very important factor in our thesis.

BLISSFUL NAIVETÉ

Despite his intelligence, his vast communication and transportation facilities, and his great storehouse of accumulated information, man as an individual and as a species behaves very much like other creatures of the earth. He hurts, gets hungry, makes love, reproduces, gets sick, and dies. He reacts to the elements of his immediate environment, for the most part disregarding all else except as a matter of some curiosity. Moreover, he tends to assume that he neither does nor can affect very much things beyond his immediate surroundings. Man gathers and utilizes the materials needed for life (and trade) similar to how a bee gathers and utilizes honey, or as a predator in the forest stocks and utilizes its prey. He takes what he can where he finds it and then moves on to new land, new oil reserves, more plentiful water supplies and fresher air, doing so without much thought of the needs of others or the condition of the area he is leaving behind. Modern man, however, exerts an influence much beyond his views about what he is doing. The actions, the decisions, and the choices made by any particular citizen seem so inconsequential both to him and to society; yet, as we know, the actions, decisions, and choices of social groups comprised as they are of individuals acting in their own self-interest exert determining influence on economic and cultural developments throughout the world. Modern man, with his freedom to select and purchase products as needed for everyday living, creates pressure points and even fracture points in market places at many locations in the world. Man's naiveté with respect to his individual influence is shown also in another outstanding way. Although the average individual assumes that decisions about international power politics are beyond him and must be left to others presumed to be more knowledgeable, he nevertheless aids, abets, condones, and sanctions pressure politics simply by earning a living in a defense plant or an industrial concern that manufactures materials used in warfare. Far from doing nothing about conditions in far away

places, modern man in his simple day-to-day living affects profoundly—even vitally—people who are totally unknown to him.
We are justified in asking, therefore, whether modern man with
his naiveté, his eagerness to earn, and with his checkbooks and
his credit cards is not too dangerous to have loose on the land.
Moods, styles, and whims can, and do, shatter whole industries;
even weaken and destroy government structures.

FREEDOM

For man the same as for beasts of the earth, freedom to move
about, to utilize resources, to leave waste, to compete, and, if
necessary, to destroy and consume one's adversaries, is a freedom
inherent in the nature of things—as it were, one ordained by
the primitive conditions of Nature. Man, however, has gone farther, assuming the right to take the adversaries' properties as
spoils of war, to enslave his people, and to rape his wives and
daughters. Modern man goes still farther by acquiring profit and
prestige by restoring that which had been so wantonly destroyed
only shortly before—doing so with a professed spirit of humanity
and magnanimity. Starting with the basic animal freedoms, man
goes much beyond other creatures in the use and application of
freedom.

If the basic freedoms to move about, to exploit, and to compete had not been a part of Nature's system, life and intellect
as we know them would not have evolved as they did. The basic
exploitive and competitive procedure made reasonable sense when
the earth, as a culture tube, had an abundance of things needed
for life. However, as the population growth curve changes from
logarithmic increase to logarithmic decrease, as it inevitably must,
and as man accelerates his exploitive procedures, the degradation
will become increasingly precipitous.

Although freedom was clearly the means by which the human
species came into existence, it will not necessarily be the means
by which long-range survival of this species can be assured.

DEMOCRACY AND FREE ENTERPRISE UNDER
CHALLENGE

Democracy and free enterprise are based on the concept of freedom—to move about, to think as one pleases, to exploit, and

to buy and sell in accord with the law of supply and demand. So consistent were such concepts with the pioneer situation that under democracy man has made a fetish of freedom, associating it with flag, patriotism, and country. In time, however, and as group living has become increasingly complex, there has been a tendency to turn away from the pattern of complete freedom. Already there are innumerable self-imposed restrictions, subsidies, preferential considerations, and large federal grants of every description. Because of subsidies to big business, and of welfare assistance to the indigent, we can say that the very rich and the very poor enjoy the benefits of socialism, while the great middle class is forced to adhere to the principles of capitalism. What is regarded as democracy at the present time is very different from that which was visualized and promoted earlier. A significant and realistic question is whether the principles of freedom and rugged individualism can have as much of a place during the coming Era of Concentration.

UNSOUND ASSUMPTIONS

By the nature of comments and questions being set forth, implications are that the human species in its groping for a way of life has made assumptions and has adopted creeds, codes, practices, and procedures that reflect poor as well as good judgments, and in doing so has revealed greed, ignorance, and ineptness in dealing with matters that affect long-range species survival. Here, attention will be given to representative wrong assumptions and to the question of how much error and inefficiency can be tolerated. The features considered will pertain to conditions in the United States primarily, but the questions raised will apply elsewhere as well.

That Population Growth Should Remain Unrestricted

Of all the assumptions made by man—tacitly or deliberately—perhaps the most significant has been acceptance of the idea that population growth should follow a natural pattern and should not be modified deliberately by human beings—that is, apart from life saving. The idea obviously emerged from the primitive situation in which man, like other creatures, multiplied in a natural environment under the influence of sexual drive—a procedure which was proving successful in providing an increasing population. As recognized already, the increase in numbers in primitive times was sufficient to enable a distribution of people to all large land areas of the earth as early as 10,000 years or more ago.

The early growth in numbers of human beings was natural—unplanned by man—but in time, a way of life and systems of economy came to be built around the idea of continuing growth and expansion. A feature obviously not known to primitive man was that his growth, like bacteria in a culture tube, was taking place according to the compound interest law and that eventually a turning point to increase rate would be reached as the required environmental sustaining elements became more scarce. As emphasized earlier, the sustaining power of the earth has been vast, and the turning point regarding limitations and restraints is only now becoming apparent. Moreover, as now evident, it is coming after a whole way of life, including ideas of freedom and free enterprise, has been created around the concept of continuing growth and expansion. Clearly, it was unsound to assume that increase in numbers of people could continue indefinitely. Either man will restrict his growth sensibly, making adjustments with respect to individual and group behavior and the production and distribution of things needed for life, or Nature will restrict it with the terrible harshness of pestilence and starvation.

That Natural Resources Are Unlimited

In a world where the materials of nature have been so bountiful, and where unrestrained exploitation has seemed to the ordinary person to make so little difference, it is difficult for most people to realize and to accept that the supply of materials, such as iron, copper and petroleum are limited. New sources of materials are, of course, being discovered and, with better technology, it is becoming feasible to process lower grade ores. But with ever-faster consumption and the increasing demands of industry, the end for various critical materials is in sight within decades and for other materials, in the not too far distant future. To assume that the supply of natural resources is unlimited obviously is unsound.

That Petroleum Energy Sources Will Last Indefinitely

Great dependence is at present being placed on petroleum as a major source of energy. Without it, most of our travel and transportation would come to a stop, lights would go out, the air in our homes and in public buildings would grow stale and become overly hot or overly cold, and much manufacturing would come to a standstill. Estimates vary about the extent of petroleum reserves, but there is little disagreement on the idea that during coming decades gasoline prices will go higher and in time become prohibitive. Nuclear, solar, tidal, and other sources of power are available to be developed, and it is reasonable to say that unless stronger effort is made to convert from dependence on petroleum to dependence on other energy sources, human society could easily be forced back to dependence on animal power for travel and for sources of fat to make candles—a step that would be difficult and probably totally impossible considering the magnitude of human needs at the present time.

That Science and Technology Will Provide

A question closely related to the one on natural resources is why so many people express such complete faith in science and technology, assuming that whatever the food, materials, or power needs of society may be, science and technology will be able to provide with adequate support and effort. Again there are reasonable explanations, although the inherent assumption is overdrawn and potentially dangerous.

Science and technology do, indeed, have a brilliant record of accomplishment with respect to food productivity, development of materials, and expanding sources of energy. In agriculture, we have seen soil, crop, and livestock improvement together with design and use of feed lot and hydroponic techniques, which have in some parts of the world caused food production to keep pace with, or even exceed population growth; in engineering we have seen the development and widespread application of combustion motors and electrical power; and in industry, as a consequence of research and development, we have seen discovery and invention that has resulted in the most remarkable improvements in efficiency of living. Moreover, we are aware of nuclear and solar energy as almost limitless sources of additional power. The accomplishment record of science and technology is remarkable and at the present time there appear to be no reasons for expecting any particular lessening of present rates of progress in these fields. But availability of food, materials, and power is not the end of the story.

Let us assume that science and technology could keep pace indefinitely with expanding human needs (which is by no means likely, limitations being what they are). We then face the population juggernaut that, with the continuation of present growth rates, will produce an inundative situation in a period shorter than the history of the United States. Partial reliance on science and technology as an answer to man's growing problem is not only justified but is a necessity; nevertheless, as a total measure such reliance would be shortsighted and unsound.

That Freedom to Exploit and Dispose Are Basic Rights

Every operative system—living or nonliving—involves input fuel or food materials, as we have seen, and also output products including residues and wastes. In living systems, the mere act of breathing in and breathing out involves these elements to some degree. The life process since the beginning has necessitated continuous consumption of raw materials and the casting off of wastes into the air, onto the land or into the waters. Such has been the design in Nature's operation, causing the early perceptive mind to accept exploitation of environmental resources and the disposal of wastes as inherent privileges. Accordingly, freedom to exploit and dispose have been accepted tacitly as basic rights, ordained by Nature, as it were, and they have been exercised by the human species the same as by all other species.

When the number of human beings was small in relation to natural abundance and human life operated like other animal life, assumption of the right to consume and dispose occurred naturally, and man in accepting and utilizing such rights occupied a natural place in Nature's system. However, with man's growing ability to save life and to utilize materials increasingly for improvement of his conditions for living, the situation has become distinctly different. Not only has man made increasing demands on the environment by increasing his numbers, but, as now so much appreciated, by creation of machines and industrial plants, which utilize vast quantities of materials and release vast quantities of waste products into the environment.

Combustion motors illustrate the character of the developmental transition. Combustion motors transform only a portion of the fuel they use into energy and, as a consequence, each automobile, truck, and airplane leaves a trail of fumes and gases—not to mention solid residues. Vehicles are concentrated on highways that extend across continents, and the concentration of both vehicles and highways is increasing. In the United States, what was recognized as localized smog over a few industrial cities only a few years ago, is now becoming contiguous over significant portions of the land. Winds and rains on occasions clear the air, but they are doing so for periods that are becoming shorter in duration. Already some cities have suffered suffocation tragedies. These are conditions that did not exist when the population was smaller, when industry was young, and when the combustion motor was new.

Of importance here is recognition that whereas the land, the sea, and the air can absorb and compensate for large amounts of human pollution, there are points of deterioration beyond which there can be no return. With multiplying cities, factories, airports, marinas, and transportation craft of every sort, the ratio of waste to waste absorption potential changes rapidly. Already we are aware of sterile lakes, rivers, bays, and estuaries, of abandoned land areas, and of the occurrence of lethal atmospheric conditions. With increasing population growth and increasing industrialization, the increased frequency of these conditions with widening influence is to be expected.

Man by means of his intelligence and his inventiveness has changed things. He has changed his position in Nature's ongoing scheme and, most importantly, he has eventually made it unsound to assume any longer that freedom to exploit and to dispose are rights to be accepted and respected.

That All Human Life Should Be Saved

A strong feature in human behavior has been the commitment to saving lives—to having as many people as could be produced naturally, and to protecting and caring for all that comprise the population. This tendency appears also to have emerged naturally from primitive and practical situations. First, there was the instinct to survive, which has been inherent in all living things since the beginning of the life process; and, second, there was in the pioneer situation a continuous need for more hands to perform the tasks required in group living as steps were taken to conquer the land, the forests, and the seas. In more recent times, more people have created more needs and therefore have been good for business, giving rise to systems of economy based on growth and expansion. In addition, more people created more voting strength.

That Procreation Should Remain Untouched and Untouchable

As part of human behavior during the pioneer period also has been the tendency to let human procreation be as free as it will under sexual compulsion and to hold large families in high esteem. These were silent or indirect ways of encouraging population growth.

Inherent in the life-saving and procreating processes, as fostered, has been a kind of goal—one not consciously expressed but nevertheless included. It is an assumption that there is virtue in achieving and accommodating the largest possible number of people on the earth. In recent times, human societies have gone so far as to make a fetish out of life saving and of resisting contraceptive practices with a religious fervor. It has been regarded as automatically the thing to do with no questions asked.

Why there is at present such a strong commitment to the saving of all crippled and weak individuals at birth, and doing so at all costs, is not easy to comprehend. Ostensibly it is done out of a sense of public duty and humanity, but it is suggested that the overly benevolent action may be accounted for in some degree by another aspect of human nature. In modern man, as we have recognized, there is a strong appetite for compassion, and the helpless or injured child provides opportunity to satisfy this appetite. This is a trait sometimes more easily recognized by others than by ourselves, as illustrated by the beggar lad in the Holy Land who said "Sir, I will gladly oblige by accepting your gift." Obviously he felt he was performing a service for which he should be compensated.

Human tendencies with respect to the saving of life is revealed further by developments in countries of the East concerning infanticide. Until fairly recently, the sacrifice of lives at birth was not uncommon in the Orient. In Japan, the word for what we in the West call "infanticide" is "*mabiki*," which, when literally translated, means "thinning" as used when one speaks of thinning the rice crop. Implied is intent to take out the weak and reduce the number of plants in such a way as to obtain the maximum crop yield. By many standards, *mabiki* would be judged a remarkably sound concept. Western colonists and missionaries, however, condemned the practice as barbaric, the step being a means of striking at the moral fiber of the people, creating guilt complexes, and thereby making them more subservient and more susceptible to control. Whether infanticide is more barbaric than creation of teeming infested ghettos, is also a moral question.

When "life" begins and when a new individual becomes a citizen entitled to the privileges of society is a fundamental question and one that has a great deal of significance in the present considerations. When a new individual becomes a citizen so that taking his (its) life constitutes a form of murder, is quite arbitrary. Some argue that "life" begins at conception, others when "life is felt" and still others when the child at birth meets certain standards of fitness.

Those who argue that all life should be saved at any cost, place themselves in an odd position. All sperm and ova constitute forms of life just as much as fertilized ova or a newborn child. Yet, as made clear earlier, it is completely impossible for all germ cells to be accommodated. Some are discriminated against. Selections are made. It is part of Nature's operational scheme that this is so. The production of excess sperm and ova has been a way of insuring that procreation will occur, and natural selection has been Nature's way of thinning to insure the best crop. By countermanding natural selection through life-saving techniques, man has removed one of Nature's most important cleansing and purifying processes with respect to species vigor.

Those who say that the act of procreation should not be influenced by the conscious effort of man are saying, at the same time, that the creation of new life should be left subject to the free play of sexual passions on a kind of hit or miss basis. This seems a strange, if not risky and dangerous procedure, in an intelligent species where sex is assuming such a major role apart from procreation. Moreover, it is a strange and inconsistent policy that condones the most grandiose life-saving steps on the one hand and on the other that the all-important step of creating life should receive so little attention comparatively.

Accepting that the present situation with respect to life saving and procreation may have arisen out of primitive and pioneer conditions relating to business, religious, missionary, colonial, and other needs, it is becoming increasingly important that we reappraise our entire philosophy with respect to this generalized field.

That the Innocence of Youth Should Be Maintained

Closely related to the matters of sex and procreation—and in a way contributing to the problems they involve—is the odd and strangely complicating practice of keeping youth totally ignorant concerning these things. Why the innocence of youth is defended so widely and so strongly as a feature of human life is one of the most perplexing elements of human behavior—and the more so since during youth the natural aspects of life are accepted with greater ease. It is difficult to think of anything even remotely comparable anywhere else in the animal kingdom. Obviously, the practice at present is maintained mostly because of custom, but there is the question of how it came to be. The practice, it is evident, did not come from primitive life, yet it appears to have existed before the pioneer period we have been considering. Indications are that early moralists of biblical times sought a means of getting at people's conscience through the creation of guilt complexes and chose to strike at man's most emotional area, condemning sex and even the knowledge of it as sinful. In any case, ignorance of sex and reproduction—two of the most important of human functions—is firmly fastened on today's society as a curse. It makes not only for personal insecurity and frustration but also for all that is bawdy in entertainment. It makes a basis for the whole field of pornography. Dealing with responsible procreation, family welfare, and population matters is doubly hard when the starting point is one of ignorance about one's most basic drives.

That Drugs Make a Useful Crutch

Although as a society we have tended to insist on no interference with Nature in the fields of sex and reproduction, we have tended at the same time to go all out in augmenting other body functions with drugs of every description—placebos, medicines, stimulants, tranquilizers, anesthetics, hallucinogens, and even poisons. We are a hooked generation as far as drugs are concerned. Most upper right- or left-hand drawers of executive and secretarial desks and most home medicine cabinets are filled with nostrums of many kinds. A few medicines are beneficial, producing an actual improvement in well being, but many are not, making a hazard or causing actual harm. Why so many smoke, drink, or inject themselves into states of mental turbulence, and why so many stoke their bodies with strange medicinals is an enigma. Nature has set the mind and the body tissues to operate in a reasonably efficient manner, and it is obvious that only the most learned people would be able to outguess Nature on matters of health and functional efficiency. Man makes odd assumptions with respect to his bodily needs.

That Higher Education Should Be for the Brilliant

In the United States we award scholarships to those who by some means acquire higher marks, and thus place more education on those with education already. The result is a widening separation between those who are more comprehending and those who are less so. One can ask, therefore, if it would not be more democratic to offer education to all to the limits of their intelligence—that is, offering education equally within the means available and doing so without discrimination with respect to intelligence.

That the Cost of Medical Care Should Go Unchecked

Modern medicine, as practiced, is capable of almost unlimited use of modern technology, and a generalized assumption is that no cost should be spared in efforts to prolong life even a few minutes. This situation, combined with a disproportionate rewarding of medical professional personnel, causes medical care to be a heavy burden on the people through taxation and to be priced out of reach of the average person who must pay his own way. The science of medicine has made remarkable progress, although the medical profession has made remarkable change without much progress in providing health care and costs have been permitted to go beyond the means of the average citizen.

That Free Enterprise Will Serve as Well During the Era of Concentration as During the Era of Expansion

The human society, it must be remembered, is only a little beyond the initiation of industrialization, which definitely is or was part of the Era of Expansion. Few make projections into the future, and few as yet are making a distinction between expansion and concentration. Since most people are impressed only by immediate and actual situations, more complexity, more congestion, more pollution, and more insurrections will be required to bring home the difference. Many, without awareness of the meaning of concentration, will argue that inasmuch as the expansionest and competitive system was good enough for our forefathers in their time, it should be good enough for us in ours.

In a spirit of inquiry, we are questioning whether free enterprise in the period ahead can have anything like the effectiveness it has had in the past. The chamber of commerce philosophy, to which we are adapted and sharply tuned, of course will bring more expansions, more growth, and more business, but with the conditions of societal complexity we face already, one is caused to wonder whether such action will not inevitably bring a disproportionate amount of restriction and insecurity—that is, unless steps are taken fairly soon to make the creation and distribution of wealth dependent on activities other than expansion and growth, utilizing a more equitable procedure. It must be remembered that the Chamber of Commerce approach is part of the pioneer philosophy, and that a different kind of economic base may be required in the period ahead if more widespread poverty is to be avoided.

That Institutionalization Is an Answer to Societal Problems

The formation of institutions is indeed a way of dealing with group problems. It is a way of financing, of fixing objectives, and of organizing to achieve goals. As indicated already, however, institutions have a way of creating new problems—some of them greater than those for which the institutions were formed to resolve. The question is whether there are ways to prevent *organization dry rot* and at the same time accomplish the purposes for which the organizations were formed.

That Fixed Laws and Charters Comprise the Best Approach to Societal Management

An underlying question is why we seek to coordinate and to direct a dynamic and ever-changing society with fixed laws and charters. The assumptions have been that problems can best be resolved and difficulties overcome by enacting laws, creating ordinances, and establishing charters, contracts and treaties, covering every conceiveable contingency. More than this, the tendency has been to say that justice is best served by resorting to previous interpretations of laws in connection with cases handled at an earlier time—that is, by precedent.

The societal organism lives, breathes, and behaves in accordance with the characteristics of systems generally. It requires fuel to keep the societal organism powered and capable of performing. By means of sense organs it is aware of the surrounding environments and by means of its overall communication system it is aware of self as an entity apart from the environments. By means of efferent pathways and motor facilities, action is taken according to needs. It is moment-to-moment adaptation that makes for meaningful and effective behavior. Consider what the coordinative function in an individual human being would be as he responds adaptively to continuously changing environmental conditions if the rules governing his behavior had been based on previous situations that were considerably different and not very explicit in the first place. With poor communication and rigid rules, is it any wonder that societal organisms are awkward, inefficient, and only partially satisfying?

Straight-jacketing with fixed laws and charters comprise a poor and only partial answer to dynamic societal problems. A question therefore is whether there are ways to get along with fewer rules and to depend on expressed good intent sealed with a tacit agreement or a hand-shake rather than stultifying documentation. A legitimate question is whether all laws and all charters of institutions should not automatically become obsolete every five years, requiring renewal and updating to fit new needs and new situations. Rejustification and updating of existing laws would make a beginning for improvement.

That Nationalism Should Be Maintained as a Way of Life

It is an amazing fact that the people of the earth have elected to build such great strength into nation states. How civilization has involved the emergence of families to tribes to states and to nations is easy enough to see, but why such great emphasis has been placed on the sovereignty of nations instead of uniting them for the common good is not as easily comprehended or explained. Based on experiences to date in settling disputes between large factions of people, the design of a system of world law should not be an overwhelming task. What we as a species have done instead has been to divide the land areas of the world into territories and have the inhabitants defend the respective territories with all the force and tenaciousness at their command. There is but a single species of human beings spread throughout the world, and already there is a high degree of interdependence among the factions; yet what is done? We insist on complete independence and play games by fixing immigration quotas, manipulating gold standards, administering foreign aid, and promoting armaments races—the latter now in increments of overkill.

In recognition of need for world integration, the United Nations was formed, but the provisions in its charter go only part way. This organization brings together people from different parts of the world and they talk together, but always in the name of their respective countries. It is distressing to hear the representatives day after day saying *my country this* and *my country that* when the great and urgent need is for spokesmen for the whole of mankind. Why is it assumed that a union of nations can do the job a world organization representing the whole people would be required to do?

Governments are formed ostensibly to serve the people, but through institutionalization, as we have seen, they soon come to rule the people—even in democratic countries. In the United States, the Government has come to consist of pyramids on pyramids of power structures whose business it is to dole out monies by means of allocations, grants, contracts, subsidies, social security, and health care programs—to mention only some. Increasingly, the lines of people from the states with hat in hand become longer and more numerous and—we may say—more degrading. True, the trend is with consent of the governed, through representation, but this provision is not preventing the tightening grip of government on the people, especially since the government increases its power by greater taxation followed by revenue sharing.

The problem first is how to operate a society with diminishing rather than increasing government influence, and second how to develop administrative facilities that would serve all the people of the human species with justice.

That Warfare Should Be Retained as an Instrument of Policy

The question here is why there is such widespread acceptance of warfare as a way of settling international disputes. This question stands very much by itself, and a response to it must be mainly in terms of man's fundamental personality design.

There are different ways that living creatures as self-organizing, adaptive, and purposive systems, can deal with each other—individually or collectively. With respect to any given individual, the premises can be that: (1) all other individuals or groups are enemies seeking opportunity to destroy one the moment there is an advantage; (2) other individuals or groups are peaceful except when they need one's possessions for food or other purposes; and (3) only those who are more powerful are one's enemies. In the case of human beings, it can be assumed as an additional alternative that other human beings are civilized and can be dealt with on the basis of reason and mutual respect.

In the jungle, and wherever life exists in the wild, it is a fairly safe assumption that other creatures or groups of creatures will not attack unless their security (including the threat of starvation) is threatened. In the case of human beings, one can assume—also with some justification—that other human beings will on occasion attack maliciously simply to destroy one's influence and power, to take one's possessions for his own use, or simply for the purpose of experiencing triumph. In this respect, human beings are different, and it is difficult to find ways of regarding the difference as an advancement.

Human beings are strange creatures. On the one hand they manifest intelligence and apply the most lofty principles of civilization in dealing with each other and, on the other, they resort to the most primitive animalistic behavior amplified with all the fiendishness and destructiveness that man has been able to invent.

Increasingly, as civilization becomes more complex, there appears to be growing unwillingness on the part of people in dealing with each other to trust intelligence and reason. Civilization as now being advanced involves elements of erosiveness.

Why we in the United States place so much dependence on warfare as an instrument of policy, is explained in part by the developmental trends and the effects of institutionalization on our defense establishments. When we were a young and revolutionary country, there was need for a military facility to hold off intrusive and domineering powers. An army was formed to protect the land and a navy to insure privileges on the high seas. Soon Marine and Coast Guard units were formed to cover intermediate situations. Later the Air Force was formed to insure dominion over the air, and then a Joint Chiefs of Staff to provide coordination. Still more recently the CIA was established to pry out the intent of presumed potential and real enemies and to subvert strategically using the most diabolical and most sophisticated clandestine methods as needed. Each organization was established as a service unit to perform a specific task, but quickly each became transformed into an institution acting in its own interest with its own *esprit de corps*, involving its own personal commitments and loyalties and having its own lobbies to insure support. War and the threats of war—real or imagined—are ways of keeping these institutions alive. These institutions are also ways of keeping warfare alive.

With the growing complexity of weaponry, there has emerged also the science-military-industrial complex that now is costing the United States taxpayer in excess of 75 billion dollars a year. Earlier, support of defense establishments coincided in large degree with national emergencies. Now, the trend is different, as illustrated by the following figures. Just prior to World War II (1940), according to Ralph Lapp (*The Weapons Culture*, 1968), the national defense expenditure was less than two billion dollars, but by the end of the war (1946) it had gone above 80 billion. By 1948, it had dropped to about 12 billion where it remained until the next national emergency. During the Korean War (1953) it shot up to 50 billion and above, where it has remained until the outbreak of the Viet Nam hostilities (1964), when it went substantially higher. Lapp has said "There has been no let down after Korea; instead, high priority was assigned to research and development, as . . . costly new weapons systems emerged. Never once has the U. S. Congress failed to fund a single major weapons system that was proposed to it and, more often than not, it has championed new arms while they were still in prospect. All in all, our nation has spent about 1 trillion dollars on its post war armaments (the interval between the Korean and Viet Nam wars)." With the welfare of literally millions of people now dependent on Pentagon-disbursed paychecks, and with so much of our educational, research, and technological development dependent on defense-justified support, it is apparent that in our time we have accepted military advancement as a way of life. Lapp summarized as follows: "It is no exaggeration to say that the United States has spawned a weapons culture which has fastened an insidious grip upon the entire nation."

The strangeness of military developments throughout the world is indicated also by the remarkable statement made some ten years ago by President Kennedy when he said, on March 4, 1960, that the world's nuclear stockpiles amount to "about 10 tons of TNT for every person on the globe."

It is becoming increasingly apparent that warfare as an instrument of policy is not only too costly but also much too dangerous. Continued reliance on it as a way of settling international disputes and of maintaining national prestige could easily prove inundative or obliterative.

That Secrecy and Espionage Are Desirable Practices

During the period since World War II there has been a strong tendency to assume that by keeping certain scientific, technical, and other information secret, special advantages of some sort would accrue to the United States. Similarly, there has been an increasing tendency to resort to and depend on the methods of spying, intrigue, and subversion, both domestically and abroad. At home there are fattening and multiplying dossiers on individuals and organizations giving someone else's views about how the subject individual or organization thinks, what they believe, and how they might be expected to behave under differing circumstances. The practice is employed not only by the military to insure against disloyalty and lack of commitment to views and programs as decided on by the controlling groups, but also by business, industry, and other kinds of establishment groups. With respect to individuals and groups abroad, the dossiers contain information about alignment with power blocks and what might be required to buy them off or subvert them.

These are strange practices in a country which, during its pioneer period, laid such great stress on individual rights, on freedom to know, on freedom of expression, and on free enterprise. They are strange practices by a country involved with humanitarian aid programs throughout the world, a primary purpose of which is to create mutual confidence and respect. There is obvious incongruity, but it is plain that the shift in philosophy and approach coincident with expanding affluence has been regarded as desirable and necessary in the national interest. Exchange of an implied attitude of mutual confidence and respect for one of suspicion and distrust is a heavy price to pay for assumed elements of security advantage. It is self-defeating and grossly degrading.

That Inflation and Armaments Comprise a Satisfactory Basis for Economic Progress

With a large and widely distributed population that is growing rapidly, and with free enterprise and an industrial economy, employment is a vital matter. Employment is the means by which the system works. By experience it is known that when unemployment exceeds five percent unrest mounts and violence increases. During the past decade and more in the United States, the problem of employment has been overcome in large measure by inflation and by investment in arms. Inflation stimulates business and pays the interest on government bonds, and investment in armament systems creates jobs all along the line. Inflation borrows on the future and excessive armaments is wasteful and artificial at a time when resource shortages are being felt increasingly. It is difficult to find a basis for expecting that this approach to sustaining a way of life can endure for long.

That Democracy Will Endure During the Era of Concentration

Democracy as a form of government and as a way of life was developed during the Era of Expansion and without doubt it served well during the pioneer period when life was simpler and the right of franchise had more meaning. In view of vast and rapid change, however, it is necessary to ask whether the success of democracy in the past necessarily guarantees continued success in the period ahead.

One generalized assumption is that since democracy worked well for our forefathers, it should also work for us. A second generalized assumption is that inasmuch as democracy is based on the concept of freedom and the enhancement of human dignity, it contains the elements essential for the best form of living, and therefore should be expected to serve appropriately in the future. Still another generalized assumption is that free enterprise as a basic element of democracy, with its features of competition and expediency, is in phase with the principles of freedom and individual expression and therefore inviolable—simply not to be questioned. However, because of the inexorable increase in societal complexity resulting from growing numbers of people and expanding technology, the trend has been just the opposite— that is, despite democratic principles, to restrict personal freedoms and to counteract free enterprise increasingly. In case of national emergencies, democratic countries resort to price control and rationing, to confined movements of the people, and to assigned work activities, thus giving up freedom and individualized action to a very large degree. Since the Era of Concentration must inevitably be a period of increasing emergency, it is to be presumed that as a people we will resort increasingly to more restrictions, more subsidies, more government grants, more public works, more social security, and the like, thus raising serious question about how much longer the democratic system with its basic principles of personal liberties and free enterprise can endure.

Democratic governments are based squarely on justice backed by a court system purporting to sift out the truth and prescribe just treatments under well-defined laws. As we know so painfully, however, the court system that served well earlier when the number of cases to be handled was much fewer and the laws were simpler and more direct, is very much obsolete and failing increasingly, thus resulting in deteriorating confidence in the system.

Democratic governments are also based on the right of franchise—the right to exercise a choice in selecting candidates to hold office and perform tasks in the public interest. Considering the present multiplicity of offices and candidates, and also the intricate and complex nature of the offices to be filled, it is probably no exaggeration to say that exercise of the right of franchise is one of the most frustrating experiences one can have. The sheer helplessness one feels as he leaves the polling booth also contributes to a deterioration of confidence in the democratic process.

Democratic governments are also based specifically on the idea of fair representation of all factions of the constituency. Yet the operation is on the basis of political parties—special interest groups, making it necessary for representatives to act in favor of the groups that elected them. Within the system as it operates, therefore, there are lobbying, pressure tactics, special protection, the condonation of strikes, monopolies, and the like. With the drift away from fair representation of all factions—partly because of the growing ponderousness of the task—there has been additional loss of confidence in governmental operation with increasing demonstrations and insurrections.

Loss of confidence in democratic government stems in particular from a growing feeling that leaders, simply because they are "in," are insensitive to changing situations and therefore hold tenaciously to traditional but outmoded procedures because they favor the "in" factions. How to restore confidence in the face of rigid traditions, powerful self-interests, and a worsening situation is today's paramount problem.

UNAVOIDABLE MAJOR CHANGE

Nineteen assumptions that underlie the life and behavior of modern man have thus been set forth. Each is representative of views commonly held and each involves features that cause the logical mind to revolt in some degree. Many other examples could have been given, but the number presented is sufficient for our purposes. Emphasis has been on the weaknesses and failures of development because this is where the problems lie.

The listing as given pertains to some of the most cherished and most universally accepted of human institutions, and under less critical circumstances it would be a sacrilege even to question them. Because of growing unrest and insecurity, however, any treatise of modern societal problems is compelled to do so and to do it as broadly and as completely as possible.

In Table 4, the 19 assumptions are compiled for more convenient reference along with the views about them given in brief.

Table 4. Assumptions Underlying Societal Behavior

	Assumption	Soundness	Consequences	Reasons for
1.	That population growth should remain unrestricted	Unsound and impossible	Disastrous if present growth rates continue	Ignorance, naiveté
2.	That natural resources are un-limited	Incorrect	Leads to erroneous judgments	Ignorance
3.	That petroleum energy sources will last indefinitely	"	Could be disastrous	"
4.	That science and technology will always provide	Unsound and unsafe	Leads to erroneous judgments	"
5.	That freedom to exploit and dis-pose are basic rights	"	Disastrous within decades	Ignorance, naiveté
6.	That all human life should be saved	Humanitarian but unrealistic	Contributes to the population problem	Naiveté
7.	That procreation should remain untouched and untouchable	Unsound and unsafe	"	Ignorance, naiveté
8.	That the innocence of youth should be maintained	Tolerable but damaging	Frustration, mistrust	Ungrounded assumptions
9.	That drugs make a useful crutch	Sometimes but usually not	Often injury and loss of stamina	Misinformation, coercion
10.	That higher education should be for the brilliant	Undemocratic	Increasing gap between the knowledgeable and the less knowledgeable	Desire to reward excellence

Table 4 (continued)

	Assumption	Soundness	Consequences	Reasons for
11.	That the cost of medical care should go unchecked	Frustrating	Poor medical and health services	Inept management
12.	That free enterprise will serve as well in the future as in the past	Unwarranted	Modification or replacement	Tradition, favorable past results
13.	That institutionalization is an answer to societal problems	Partially correct	May be self-defeating	Internal workings
14.	That fixed laws and charters comprise the best approach to societal management	"	Often inadequate due to obsolescence and lack of applicability	Adherence to custom and tradition
15.	That nationalism should be maintained as a way of life	Sound if it serves the people	Results in power politics which now is too dangerous	Lack of maturity
16.	That warfare should be retained as an instrument of policy	Suicidal	Species extinction	Primitive tradition
17.	That secrecy and espionage are desirable practices	Degrading	Mistrust between individuals and factions of people	Decadent and unprincipled behavior
18.	That inflation and armaments comprise a satisfactory basis for economic progress	Totally unsound	Balanced terror and chaos. Disastrous in time	Desperation and naiveté
19.	That democracy will endure during the Era of Concentration	Risky	Possible revolution	Blind confidence based on past performance

Each assumption as stated involves questions regarding suitability, appropriateness, and reliability in dealing with the problems they are intended to resolve. Taken collectively, and including as they do some of the most basic precepts of civilized living, they tend to shake one's confidence in leaders of a system that condones them and indeed, in the people who support them. The alarm that emerges, however, is based on more than loss of confidence; it is based on fear of the seeming inexorableness of at least certain trends.

The assumptions of Table 4 divide naturally into two classes: those that are faulty and constitute an obvious hindrance to social progress, and those that are potentially disastrous. Among the latter are unrestrained population growth, unrestricted exploitation and disposal, inflation and armaments as the main economic base, warfare as an instrument of policy, and nationalism with balanced terror as a way of life.

Quite obviously, human society is sitting on a time bomb due to be detonated sooner or later by any one of a number of entities. Change of some major sort quite soon seems inevitable. Either population growth will be restrained and the unsound operational policies shifted, or the natural forces will reach zero on the countdown. Going either direction—that is, intelligent management or seat-of-the-pants management leading to catastrophic disruption—will be a major change.

Chapter 10

Jet-propelled Man and the Earth as a Closed System

In preceding chapters, we have come close to concluding that the human species is not only in an extremely precarious position, teetering between oblivion and ascendence, but also that human beings are essentially powerless to insure a constructive course. What then is to be expected? Is our period really any more precarious than critical periods faced heretofore? Is there really the possibility of passing a point of no return? What are minimum requirements for man's survival and advancement in our time? Are they essentially different from the requirements at earlier times? What will modern man, with his restless spirit, find tolerable as a minimum? In an effort to assure a positive course of development, is it necessary to think only in terms of restraints and a forfeiting of privileges? Are minimum requirements for constructive advancement actually achievable within the limitations already fastened on us? At the present stage of development, is there any other way for human advancement than by means of planned and managed global ecology? These are the kinds of questions to be considered here.

COMPARATIVE SERIOUSNESS OF THE PROBLEM

Risks and catastrophies have been numerous in man's history, yet somehow the human species has always been able to muddle through, multiply, and advance. Now, in the midst of widely distributed affluence—perhaps the highest ever—question is being raised not only about the problems of growing complexity but, more particularly, about the possibility of impending human failure—the actual loss of civilization or of the human species itself. Certainly everyone with any sensitivity at all sees and appreciates the growing smog and pollution problems, and everyone inevitably feels the oppressive effects of growing congestion; but, the average person continues to ask: "Are these difficulties any more than temporary inconveniences to be resolved in time by technology? Are they any more serious than problems the human species has faced before? Are they not the price we must expect to pay for growing improvement? Is there any reason why they cannot be resolved as other problems have been resolved by investment of effort and money when the chips are down and it is really necessary to do so? What is all the panic about disaster? What, if anything, is different about today's period? Is the fate of the next generation really being determined by decisions made by the present generation? Is human society actually being forced by developments to plan ahead in unprecedented ways?

There are some answers.

Never before—that is, never before in the present century—has the human species been without a land frontier. Previous to this century there have always been new land areas to which people could migrate and make their homes. There are, of course, large land areas yet unoccupied, but none that are unowned and free to habitation. Being without a land frontier is a new situation. It changes man's opportunities. It necessitates a different outlook on life.

Never before has there been a world population of more than three billion people, and never before has there been a world population growth rate of two percent per year, causing a total population doubling every half century or less. With a continuation of existing growth rates, as stressed already, it would be but a matter of centuries—not millenia, but centuries—before all of the unoccupied land areas, including skyscrapers, floating islands, and space under the seas, would become occupied and congested —a kind of thing that cannot happen for many reasons that are obvious. The actual necessity of a declining birth rate is also something new. Realizing that the inevitable slowing of growth would not only affect business as visualized and idealized by the chamber of commerce adherents and most, if not all, of the rest of society, it would affect the whole economic approach and our entire philosophy of life. The struggle would not be for accommodation of the maximum achievable number of souls on the earth but instead for a good life involving a comparatively fixed population. The watchwords would not be "growth" and "expansion," but "stability" and "quality." Struggle to attain the good life without the concepts of "more," "bigger," and "faster" would indeed be different.

Never before has the rate of resource utilization been so great, and never before has there been such a widening gap between the "have" and "have not" factions of people and between the "have" and "have not" countries. Industrialization has indeed made its amazing positive contributions to the affluent life, but very disproportionately. In industrialized countries, the land, the forests, the mountains, the waterways, and the seas are being pressed for the resources they can provide. By means of reclamation and conservation measures some land, forest, and water areas are not only being maintained in productivity, but are forced to function at maximum levels, as done in hydroponic and feed-lot operations. In case of nonrenewable resources, there is, of course, no replacement, and already the voraciousness of industry is causing much lower-grade ores and less productive sources of many kinds to be worked. With a growing scarcity of raw materials in industrialized countries, the tendency has been to purchase from less-developed countries. Because of the wealth created by industry, such purchasing is possible and a mutual advantage is seen—that is, one that is immediate. What happens, however, is that the birthright of less-developed countries is sold without the benefit of gains more permanent than those provided by commodity goods that money can provide. Despite full compensation plus pump-priming provided additionally by foreign aid, subsistence countries improve little. The tendency is for population growth to absorb and counteract the gains, causing the subsistence conditions to remain. Moreover, with more and more people depending on foreign aid, the resources of donor countries are drained away increasingly and they are made subject to the charge of great inhumanity if ever any of the support is withdrawn. The trend at first is one of widening gaps between the "have" and "have not" countries and then a generalized degradative balancing caused by dwindling resources in donor countries. This is a new situation also. Increasingly, there is dependence on science and invention to counteract the resource shortage situation, and increasingly there is need for a philosophy and an approach for dealing with the multiplying and spreading subsistence populations.

Never before has there been a time when oppressive and threatening smog hangs like a pall over vast urbanized and industrial areas for weeks on end, and never before have large numbers of rivers, lakes, and estuaries become sterile and thus unable to support life. Never before have our soils been so contaminated with poisonous insect and weed killers and never before have our food chains in the oceans and on the land been so severely threatened by man-made agricultural and industrial contamination. The air, the water, and the soils are places where things live, and they are vital to the human species as it has come to operate. The air, the water, and the soils, as they have existed on the earth, are comprised of mixes of elements to which life has become adapted. These proportions with respect to some elements and some operative systems are also fairly delicate. Shifts need not be extreme to make the conditions incompatible with life. Heretofore, distortions in the life-sustaining features of the environment have been adequately compensated by natural processes and caused to disappear. Now, however, with smog extending from the urbanized areas across the deserts and the plains and with poisonous wastes accumulating in the oceans, the natural processes are being pressed to a point of no return. Already many lakes and rivers have become sterile as far as support of vital food chains is concerned. The natural reactions involved are of the sort that the swing from life-supporting to nonlife-supporting could become rapid once the balance has been pressed too far. These kinds of problems are new. They did not exist to any threatening degree before the period of billions of people and the period of industrialization.

Never has there been such a morass of harassment in everyday living involving the complexity of traffic and transportation, to say nothing of the complications encountered in dealing with matters of health, medical care, schools, legal problems, insurance, taxes, and the like. Although difficulties are being overcome in some areas, they are becoming more intense in a great many others. Life at all stages has been complicated, but the level of technical complexity now faced is unprecedented.

There are, of course, improvements and advancements of many kinds to offset the deteriorating situations. Never has there been such an accumulation of technical know-how for food production and for the creation of other commodities needed for life; never have there been so many skilled hands to do the work; and, it seems safe to say, never have people been more eager to advance the human cause—that is, as long as it does not interfere with precious tradition or the opportunity to earn. Much more stress could be laid on the existent and expanding positive aspects of life; but, it is to be remembered that the main objective of this text is to recognize and deal with the intensifying predicaments coming from man's development and especially his advancement as an intellectual being.

The negative and the plus factors contributing to man's welfare may be compared in the following way. Let us again suppose that the production of food and other commodities needed for life were not a problem and would be plentiful irrespective of the number of people making demands. We are aware already that with continuing population increase rates, standing room in actuality and reality will become a problem in a matter of a few centuries. We are cognizant of the fact that environmental pollution problems already exist and threaten to become critical or disastrous in localized areas any time from now on into the future.

Going further, we are aware of increasingly heroic efforts to overcome the environmental problems. At the same time we know that these efforts are faltering and are limited. Let us suppose that all industrial exhaust stacks were adequately capped and that all automobile, truck, and airplane exhaust outlets were adequately controlled. This would make an enormous difference—at least temporarily. The beneficial result at best, however, would be a transitory reprieve. With continued increase in the number of people together with the livestock needed to sustain human beings, we would in time reach the stage when people exhaust would become a limiting factor—that is, when the atmosphere would become so completely contaminated with expired air that ventilation would have little effect. Continuously, we must remember that we live in a closed system and there is a limited amount of atmosphere just as there is a limited amount of mineral resources or agricultural land. When there are no longer enough trees to provide the oxygen needed for animal life, and when a disproportionate amount of carbon dioxide resulting from animal (human) respiration combined with noxious fumes, the point of no return will have been passed, and such a point could be reached in a few centuries—that is, after a few more population doublings—even if industrial and machine exhausts were not a problem.

What we have operating, irrespective of food or industrial problems is a race between population growth on the one hand and the energizing efforts of science and technology to stave off growing degradation and possible catastrophy, with the outcome to be decided in a century or so at the most, and probably within a few decades. It is clear, and without equivocation, either that population growth will stabilize at or near zero fairly soon, or that science and technology will become inundated and overwhelmed. It is no longer a question of whether drastic change will occur, but rather of how soon the effects of such change will be felt strongly. If population growth remains essentially as at present, the change will be of one type and if it is sensibly controlled, it will be of quite a different type.

Let us theorize further.

Suppose on the one hand that population growth rates are not reduced. What then would be the expected changes in the environment, in business, and in human relations?

TRANSITION STAGES

With respect to environment, as countries emerge from the pioneer conditions of abundance of fresh air, pure water, and green plains and forests, the following conditions might well occur.

Stage 1. We would expect to see occasional cities, roadways, and factories across the land that make little difference in the abilities of the atmosphere, the waterways, and the natural green growth areas to compensate for comparatively small contaminations or losses that occur.

Stage 2. In time we would expect to hear of an unusual condition of gaseous wastes hanging over an important city for a few days, of an occasional river, or lake failing to produce fish, and of occasional dust storms over cultivated areas. We would expect these occurrences to attract transitory attention and that essentially no action would be taken.

Stage 3. With more time—say a few years—we would expect a pall of irritating smog to appear over more urbanized industrial areas and last for increasingly longer periods of time. We would expect to hear of sportsmen and fishermen complaining about loss of water, field, and forest productivity. At this time, we would expect to hear also of steps to stock the streams and lakes with fish, of dam and irrigation projects to save and develop the land, and of intensified hydroponic and feed-lot developments to stoke selected chromosome combinations in an effort to compensate for losses in natural productivity and for the growing demands.

Stage 4. With still more time—again a few more years—we would expect to see continuous and ubiquitous smog, recognized as contributing to increased hospitalization and earlier deaths. At this stage, we would expect to see people, even if grudgingly, giving up agricultural areas, parks, and outdoor recreational facilities for more factories, more roads, more airports, and more shopping areas, doing so with spreading fear and frantic efforts to counteract the degradative trends.

Stage 5. We would expect to hear crys of "too late," "we should have started sooner."

Stage 6. We would expect to see, if we were lucky and thus among the living, worldwide decimation due to massacres, starvation, and disease, a serious setback in civilization, and a new start with attention to population growth rates.

Concerning business, we might see changes that coincide with the six environmental stages indicated. In briefer form, they may be listed as including the following: increasing wealth and affluence during the Era of Expansion (dependent in part on population growth), permissive inflation to insure industrial expansion and thereby full employment of a growing population, limited and piecemeal efforts to control inflation, a consequent stockmarket turn down but with confident feelings that the "recession" would be temporary, some temporary upturns but with continued downward trends as the inflationary weapons culture tightens its grip, and finally, at Stage 6, a precipitous collapse with resulting failure of investment, insurance, and social security capabilities.

Concerning interpersonal relations, the transformation expected concurrently would be as follows: During the pioneer period a significant degree of mutual trust and respect within factions with disputes being settled quickly and in accordance with existing situations, and during the period of growing concentration, increasing mistrust, strikes, demonstrations, and disillusionment, leading to arming in the homes, increasing insurrection, worldwide raiding, and generalized civil war.

The above are speculations, but the early phases in each case have been experienced already. The trends projected are in phase with present population trends and with the existent unsound assumptions, ignorance, naiveté, and extended self-interest now characteristic of human behavior. There is no question about what will happen to population growth rates. They will come down—inevitably—and fairly soon, simply because there is no way for them to be sustained at present levels for more than a few more doublings. That which will make the difference between the loss or survival of civilization, is whether population growth will be brought down by intelligent management or by the harsh and decimative procedures of Nature. On the basis of established trends and tendencies, the degrading harsh pattern will occur—but this need not be the case. Mankind has the capabilities and the qualifications required to avert the catastrophe foreseen with such certainty, but the necessary steps would carry much beyond the consideration of population size. Just to live with a reasonably fixed population would in itself result in or require a much modified philosophy of life, a much changed value system and a much augmented approach to economic progress.

SOCIETAL PROGRESSION

In mathematics and engineering, *potentiation* is defined as the type of function from which field intensity, potential, or equilibrium is derived (see Figure 28). Potentiation can be used more generally with the same meaning and in connection with human behavior. Potentiation is a means of achieving a new state—a new level of organization. Potentiation is the process of achieving efficacy, strength, and power through response to interacting forces and the establishment of equilibria. Potentiation underlies organization leading to higher levels of complexity and capability, and it underlies disorganization leading to lower levels of functional action. Potentiation underlies individual organism behavior, societal operation, and ecosystem function. Robert Ardrey

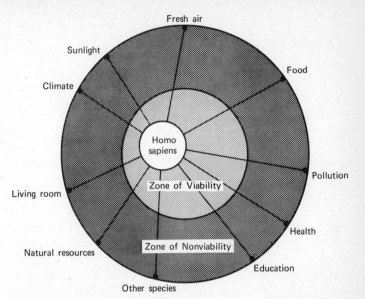

Fig. 28. Potentiation. Multiple vectors affect a species of organism within a *Zone of Viability*. When the species is drawn by some influence beyond the favorable environment, it reaches the *Zone of Nonviability*.

has written about Social Contract—the mechanism by which organisms come to accept each other, thereby establishing status and societal working arrangements. Potentiation includes Social Contract but goes beyond. It is a process of seeking balances, and it applies generally in Nature.

In earlier chapters, insight was derived from looking at organisms, including human organisms in terms of operative systems with differing levels of complexity. The approach can be utilized also to gain impressions of requirements for societal behavior under differing environmental conditions and in the period ahead. Figure 29 sets forth some thoughts.

For purposes of discussion, three levels of societal organization and governance are indicated. The first is represented by the family or tribe where the number of people is comparatively small, where leadership emerges naturally because of physical

Organization	Behavioral Response	Societal Form

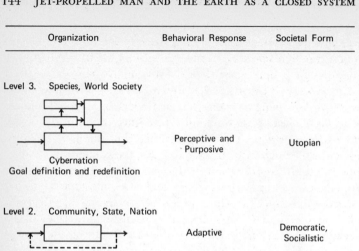

Level 3. Species, World Society

Cybernation
Goal definition and redefinition

Perceptive and Purposive — Utopian

Level 2. Community, State, Nation

Automation
Self–organization

Adaptive — Democratic, Socialistic

Level 1. Families, Tribal Groups

Cause and effect action
Stimulus–response

Reflexive — Authoritarian

Fig. 29. Social development profile.

strength, intelligence, or seniority, where there are few if any laws, and where most often there is a kind of authoritarian control. Because the group is small, communication is not a problem. Each group member can be, and usually is, aware of other people's needs and problems and even what they are thinking. Issues are settled very much as they arise by authoritarian decree and by force if necessary. Actions and reactions tend to be reflexive and the system is usually of the simple through-put type. The operative pattern, for smaller groups, is fairly efficient—that is, as long as there is a reasonable amount of mutual good intent.

The second level of societal organization and governance is that represented by communities, states, and nations where the number of people involved is in the thousands or millions, where communication is poor and it is impossible for different factions to know the conditions and needs of other factions. It is also where the different factions are dependent on a common security and on common sources of materials needed for life. When large groupings of people are involved, governance may be authoritarian, as in the case of Level 1, but it also may be democratic or socialistic, involving the selection of leaders by appointments or by means of elections of different types. Since communities, states, and nations have no way of providing continuous moment to moment coordination of the factions for the common good, as is done in case of coordination of the parts of the human body, resort is made to regulations, rules, and laws, most of which are restrictive but some of which may provide special privileges decided on in different ways. In some instances, provision of the special privileges is done with the intent to be fair, but more often it is done to satisfy self-interest pressure groups. Despite heroic humanitarian efforts to provide truly democratic governments, the effort has been only partially satisfying at best, and the reasons are fairly obvious. Consider again the behavior of a human being if operation of the different organ systems and the different body parts were not coordinated in the common interest of the whole organism. Awkwardness, stammering, and blundering action would be the result with an effort made to muddle through by any means. Such is the action of societal groups at Level 2.

As we know, the beautifully coordinated and coherent behavior of a human being—say a diver, a skater, or an orator—comes from communication and control on a continuous basis, and the question is whether human societal organisms can be operated in the same way. This would be Level 3, and it would consist of a through-put system with continuous moment-to-moment goal definition and redefinition as needed for dealing with problems and in the most effective manner possible at the time.

THE EARTH AS AN ECOSYSTEM AND WHO GETS THE LIFELINE

As emphasized, the earth is an ecosystem—a closed ecosystem. There are limits to the earth's dimensions, to the earth's resources, and to the earth's carrying capacity. The earth's operation involves potentiation that enables life, including human life. The human species, by means of its naturally evolved intellect, is creating a preferential position for itself. By working its will, the human species preserves or exterminates other species—in actuality, it makes a decision concerning which species will be encouraged to live and which will be caused to die and, by selective breeding, it even creates new species or strains. Moreover, by following primitive and traditional tendencies, the human species is struggling for the maximum attainable number of people on the earth. Because of natural limitations, and because of uncompromising natural laws, Nature is beginning to blow the whistle on human irrepressiveness. In the vast sea of competing interests, it is a question of who gets the life line—of whose rights and whose freedoms get the green light. Certainly it is impossible for the chamber of commerce adherents and the conservationists to have it at the same time. There is no way to have urbanized communities with supermarkets, asphalt strips, airports and factories, and natural areas with parks, pure air and green grass, in the same locations.

LIMITS OF ADAPTABILITY

Clearly a choice must be made between continuing exploitation with growing squalor and saner living with improving conditions, and the question is whether the human species—even with its intellect and ability to understand—is either in a position or is able to choose for the positive course.

The momentum for growth and expansion—and for acquisition of wealth and power—at the expense of the environment is strong, and the supporting philosophy is deeply ingrained. It is so strong in "in" groups (those in positions of influence and good income) that there is question whether reason can again prevail. The human species obviously thinks of itself as here to stay. It is here because it fought its way up against perilous odds, conquering the forests, the lands and the seas, exploiting as much as necessary. It is unlikely that human society will cave in on exploitation for seemingly sentimental reasons about sunshine and fresh air, or even because of a few disasters. People generally abhor suffocating fumes and putrid streams, but they are not about to give up their food crops, their automobiles, their steel plants, their copper smelters and their oil refineries—perhaps not even slightly. Everyone can see that mutual trust and respect characteristic of the pioneer era, Level 1 on the Social Development Profile, has given way to the abandon and disregard characteristic of Level 2 on this Profile—abandon and disregard, which includes widespread corruption in business, industry, and government, generalized deception in advertising, thieving in the homes, stores, and on the streets, growing insurrection on the part of minority and "out" groups, and resort to drugs of every description as a means of escape. Often the tendency is to say that the economy is strong enough to absorb this amount of corruption and even more. Few are able to make meaningful and reliable projections of trends and thus foresee impending degradation and catastrophe.

With Nature's inexorable forces taking command increasingly, there is little basis for expecting that the human species can muddle through for much longer. Furthermore, with man's sagging moral stamina, there is little basis for expecting that the human species will be able to extricate itself from the intensifying degradative spiral.

Chapter 11

Demand for and the Price of Utopia

We recognize that because of Nature's inexorable demands, some aspects of man—his nature, his values, his assumed prerogatives, or his behavioral conduct—will change extensively in the near future, by Nature's command if not by human choice. In a finite world there are limits beyond which it is impossible to go. As we have seen, Nature's rules on such matters are uncompromising and there can be no equivocation. At the same time it is necessary to accept that man also has demands—some requirements or conditions without which life would not be worthwhile and would not continue.

In any treatise of the type we have under way, it is necessary to weigh and evaluate the opposing requirements and to formulate views about probable outcome. The questions to be considered here are Nature's baseline requirements, man's baseline requirements, and which most likely will be met, taking into account man's ability to accept and cope with forced change, the tenuous course of civilization, and the necessity for and the demands of Utopia.

NATURE'S REQUIREMENTS OF MAN

If man as a species entity is to remain a part of Nature's operative scheme, it is quite clear from a priori evidence that the opportunist approach of the past will of necessity be replaced by more realistic and more carefully directed potentiation—much of it on a global basis.

Realistic potentiation at the outset would mean population size compatible with the availability of resources. This would not necessarily mean a fixed population, but it would mean numbers of people in harmony with acceptable standards and levels of living as permitted by the earth on a longer as well as a shorter term basis. It would be a kind of *mabiki* insuring the most efficient and most satisfying human crop yield. Stabilization of population growth rates at substantially lower levels, in turn, would call for certain fundamental changes in philosophy about societal operation and especially employment of the system of free enterprise. The creation of new business and wealth would of necessity have to be on a basis other than population growth as it has been to such a considerable extent in the past. Such change would not be impossible, of course, for there are many approaches that could be used as the basis for creating and distributing wealth, but it would mean turning away from growth in the pioneering sense, which yet remains so firmly fixed as a basis for human development.

Realistic potentiation would require yielding completely on warfare as an instrument of public policy and on power politics as such. Warfare as the ultimate authority is now so much of a threat to the whole species that it no longer can be contemplated with any sanity. Pyrrhic victories offer no gains. They involve no glamour, no glory, and no power advantages. Wars today are neither winnable nor conclusive, as the stalemates in Korea, Vietnam, and the Near East indicate, or they are catastrophic as illustrated by World Wars I and II. On the basis of experience since World War II, it can be said that major wars have given way to smaller wars, and that the absorbing game of international power politics is played more with armaments races in terms of multiples of overkill. Because of the risk of obliteration, total war is of necessity being given up; but, there is also another, and perhaps equally compelling reason why this is being done. Warfare is the most voracious of man's enterprises in the consumption of resources. With the existing risk of obliteration and the growing shortages of resources throughout the world, it is to be expected that even the armaments interplay will drop in priority and be favored or tolerated less and less.

Because of dependence of so many millions of people on so-called defense activities, yielding on warfare and armaments will also affect the economy profoundly—as much as and perhaps even more than stabilization of population size would do. It would be possible to shift the economic base, turning in this case from extravagent arms expenditures to support of domestic programs, but this also would mean turning from a firmly fixed and deeply ingrained practice. In the United States, taxpayers have been willing to support large-scale expenditures to counteract threats from without, be they real or imagined, but only modest amounts for schools, hospitals, housing, and public works.

Realistic potentiation would require relaxation on commitments to nationalism—a deemphasis on fanatical patriotism and emphasis on *human unity* or species unity instead. Such will be required as armament support declines, but it will be required for a more basic reason. Since the world is now a neighborhood and the various geographic human factions are so specialized and so interdependent, it is difficult and essentially impossible for any one faction to stand in isolation. Struggle for factional dominance in one area or another no longer makes sense. The problem now is one of species survival and not merely one of survival of national factions.

The indigenous elements of population growth, destructive potential and interdependence are combining to make an impelling requirement that man change significantly from at least some of his cherished traditions and modes of conduct, if he wishes to have a continuing place in Nature's grand scheme. There appears to be little room for equivocation on these matters. Nature will require them.

MAN'S REQUIREMENTS OF NATURE

If human beings as individuals are to have the incentive to remain a part of Nature's scheme—that is, to be and to remain alive—there are certain minimal requirements to be recognized. These are requirements or conditions to be matched and related to Nature's requirements for continuing participation in the overall scheme.

As noted earlier, man has instincts to survive and reproduce. Had it been otherwise, the species would not have come into being. These are fundamental and they are necessary for continuing participation. Man also functions in ways to make life more satisfying to himself—that is, to provide *identity, stimulation*, and *security*, the basic motivational elements identified by Ardrey (*The Territorial Imperative*, 1966). As noted also, there are instincts or drives to work, to own, to learn, to explore, to invent, to create, to exert an influence, to be daring and to love. Work dignifies a man. By means of it he accomplishes; more particularly, in his own eyes and the eyes of others, he earns a right to the privileges of society. Ownership or possession, whether it be of a talent or item of property, gives identity. It aids in making man more than just another individual or thing. Being a creature of intellect, the instinct to learn, to explore, to invent, to create, and to better one's lot, follow naturally—and, it appears, inevitably. Even the instinct to love and to be loved acts along with the others to provide stimulus and security. As stressed earlier, these are the features that make man stand out as a species. They make the psyche and provide motivation. Remove any one of them and a beginning is made in removal of the essence of man. Remove all of them and man ceases to exist. They are requirements for man's existence; they are requirements for man's identity as a species.

But what about competition and daring—the elements that provide stimulation? Man, like other creatures, exerts an influence, thereby creating some element of incentive just by existence; but, being a creature of intellect, invention, and creativity, man, in order to stand well in his own eyes and the eyes of others with intellect—indeed to derive personal satisfaction—must exert an influence much beyond that of identification alone. Man by his nature and because of the nature of his environment, as he exists in it, is impelled to compete and be daring—if necessary going so far as to destroy an adversary by ridicule or superior strength. Through competition and daring, man exerts more influence, adds to personal identity, and thus betters his lot. By employing almost completely opposite tactics, man seeks satisfaction also by being compassionate and having concern for others. Competition, daring, and compassion are drive traits that contribute along with others to make up the total human personality.

Society, like individual man, has attributes or qualities essential for its existence in Nature's scheme. Only one such attribute will be used to illustrate the point. It is the action steps to organize and regulate. Without communication and control (governance) social groups of any consequence could not exist. Societal management and institutionalization in some degree are indispensable elements despite weaknesses and inherent hazards. It is thus evident that efforts to overcome man's growing predicaments by modulation or redirecting instinctual drives, or by taking away the opportunity to organize and to function as social groups, would accelerate instead of decelerate the process of degradation.

The indigenous elements of identity, stimulus, and security combine to cause species man to resist at least some of the changes inexorably demanded by Nature. Nationalism, which fits awkwardly in Nature's scheme, provides boundary lines that give a basis for the most energetic and sometimes disruptive disputes, and warfare provides a means for the most intense stimuli. It has been in warfare that man has risen to his greatest heights and to his greatest glory. Some of the most popular motion pictures and television shows are those that deal with violence in the streets, in the air, and on the seas. Westerns, naval battles, and airforce engagements are run over and over again. Even children's cartoons and science fiction utilize combat as a basic theme for entertainment. Nationalism and warfare, it seems safe to predict, will be defended with the greatest tenaciousness.

MATTERS ON WHICH MAN COULD YIELD BUT PROBABLY WILL NOT

If, in our efforts to strike at the roots of man's enlarging predicaments and paradoxes, we go beyond the uncompromising conditions of Nature, the instinctive drives that characterize man distinctively as man, and the elements that make social groups possible, there are man's codes, values, and practices. These are less rigidly based and conceivably could be modified and augmented in such a way as to offset and correct in some degree for the growing difficulties.

Man could take a giant leap out of the past into the present by accepting the Era of Concentration as different from the Era of Expansion. Man could look at the signs of change and adapt his aspirations, laws, and habits accordingly.

Man could look at the pressures of population on the earth's sustaining power and yield on the widely accepted view that birth rates should remain untouched and untouchable. Many people practice birth control, but only as a matter of importance to themselves and their families. This kind of restraint, of course, affects birth rates, but in itself it is not enough. More particularly, it is in no way related to public policy or to what is regarded as desirable in the common, or group, interest. Two children per couple are required to maintain the population at existing levels —that is, assuming death rates to remain constant. Actually, the number is nearer 2.5 since some people do not marry and since some couples do not have children. If a government—for instance, the United States—did nothing more than to remove tax exemptions on the third, fourth, and additional children in families, this would be a declaration of policy. It would say to people everywhere that struggling to have the maximum attainable number of children is not in the public interest. More particularly, it would say that what is done at the family level with respect to procreation is basically important to the whole of society, and that this aspect of life must be considered along with family desires. With change in societal needs regarding numbers of people, as determined on the basis of studies by qualified analysts, a government could speak clearly to the people about procreative responsibilities simply by adjusting tax and tax exemptions. Taxation, of course, is only one of various approaches to population management.

Regarding the possibility that a declaration of public policy on population growth will be made any time in the near future in the United States, we offer the opinion that it is most unlikely. Most voters cling to the pioneer-capitalistic ethic of growth as the main means for assuring affluence. Similarly, most people with voting privileges think little beyond a few days or a few years at most. Candidates, therefore, must act in accordance with prospects of immediate gain. Most people do indeed see the growing smog and pollution problems but seldom relate to it in any significant way. They tend to view pollution only as something a little out of hand that can be handled adequately by technology in a few years' time. Seldom does one hear a question raised as to whether it would be possible for technology, even with unlimited support, to keep pace with a problem that is compounding the way population is doing. That the procreative steps taken now—this year—will go a long way toward determining smog and pollution conditions 25 to 30 years hence seldom enters anyone's mind.

Man could yield on the generally accepted view that warfare as an instrument of public policy should be maintained. Man is well schooled in methods of settling international disputes without resort to wholesale decimation. A system of world law exists in some measure already and all that would be required to give it effectiveness is a police force sufficient to insure its decisions. Developing a world police force would be such a natural step at the present stage of societal evolution and not too difficult to accomplish, but taking the steps to do so appears extremely unlikely. Warfare is traditional, and therefore bears sanction. Not only does it provide great stimulus, it is ritualized. It has its own rules for killing, for the treatment of prisoners, and for dealing with the spoils of war. At the present time one hears of no expressed desire either to strengthen the United Nations or to replace it with a stronger world facility.

Man could yield on the overly extravagant arms race thereby conserving resources to a very significant degree, but arms production is needed for employment, and employment at the present stage usually takes precedence over conservation.

Man could yield on the intense commitments to nationalism by stressing human unity, international law, a single monetary system, a single system of weights and measures, a universal langauge, and the like. However, commitment to unifying influences appears unlikely simply because of threats to existing poles of influence. Small, smug "in" groups here and there with power in their hands are not about to have their kingdoms invaded by conservationists and practitioners talking about problems "in" groups cannot see from their vantage points, or do not care to see.

Man could yield on the use of poisonous insecticides and weed killers, on unsightly junkyards, on putrid and inhumane feed lots, on contaminating refineries, paper mills, smelters, and so on, but he is unlikely to do so—at least for awhile. These are means of earning a livelihood, and at the present stage the right to earn a living tends to have precedence over action taken to offset risks to the health and welfare of the whole population, or to insure livable conditions a few years or a generation hence.

Man could yield on intoxicating, tranquilizing, and hallucinating drugs, but he probably will not because of the euphoria and escape so often considered preferable to reality.

Man could yield on a large number of ideas and practices, including outdated laws, encrusted institutions, obsolete judicial and penal systems, inefficient election and voting systems, irrational welfare systems, confusing sexual taboos, and conflicting religious dogmas. Yielding on any or all such matters in some degree would alleviate pressures and restore faith in man's ability to manage his affairs. Anything more than token action on social policy, however, is extremely unlikely with respect to the steps that man is likely to take willfully for improvement of his social welfare. There is no tradition for it. Very few people are qualified to serve as spokesmen for mankind and there are few opportunities for such. Those who attempt reform often are regarded as suspect, held in contempt, and ridiculed.

THE BASIC NATURE OF MAN

Man is a strange creature and he is a mixture of things; he is different things at different times. On the one hand, man has qualities of honesty, integrity, kindliness, sportsmanship, forbearance, and mercy and, on the other, he has qualities of dishonesty, irresponsibility, disregard, and bestiality.

In family and home group situations where there is mutual dependence, affection, tradition, and expected standards of conduct, man's better aspects are revealed—usually; he tends to be a reasonably stable and dependable creature. Moreover, by means of both domestic and foreign aid welfare services programs, man's benevolent and humanitarian characteristics together with his willingness to share and sacrifice, are shown to extend much beyond the home group environments, especially when there is solid home group, church, or government encouragement for it. But how does man in the raw behave? How does he behave when the lid is off and the restraints of civilization are removed? How does he behave when he is entirely on his own like a wild animal in the desert, on the plains, or in the forest?

We know man's behavior in conditions of panic. When menacing fires have broken out in public buildings, people irrespective of status or station trample each other to death in an effort to save themselves. The law of the jungle prevails. The instinct to survive predominates over all of the humanitarian tendencies of civilization.

We know man's behavior in time of war. In war anything goes. It is when people get shot in the back. It is when national monuments and natural forests are wantonly demolished. It is when people's homes are destroyed. It is when women and children who get in the way are obliterated. It is when men cheat on their wives and create bastard children without regard. It is when nurses and secretaries become prostitutes. It is when everybody cheats on the black market. It is when everybody steals—a little, if not a lot.

We know man's behavior when he has an advantage. In America we have seen the settler obliterate and exterminate the Indian, driving his remnants onto some of the most God-forsaken and barren land in the world. In America we have seen plantation owners, mining magnates, and shippers actually enslave other human beings. In America we have seen, and continue to see, property owners milk tenants and migrant workers for the last ounce of sustenance. In America we have seen what people do when they have a decisive weapon, using it to destroy women and children, homes, shrines, and properties irrespective of military significance.

We know man's behavior in oppressed and overcrowded conditions. Out of resentment, people who have little to lose, pillage and burn; and, out of a feeling about fairness, people who have something to lose scream for law and order.

We know man's behavior in polite society. He stands his grounds and takes every possible advantage. He utilizes every possible loophole under the law to avoid prosecution or to evade taxes. Commonly, people seek benefits under the law by means of subsidies, special protection, and special advantages; commonly people milk insurance companies for the last drop; and people generally take advantage of the other guy's weaknesses—in business and in love. With the growing pressures of society, more people are arming in their homes and in their automobiles, thus preparing to take the law into their own hands—when the time comes.

Most people have a breaking point and all, it seems necessary to say, are corruptible in some degree. Few can withstand torture to the point of death. Some are so unprincipled that they yield easily to temptation. Few people can withstand bribes—inducements for which a favor is done in return, especially if under conditions of heavy blackmail. When the ante is high enough in terms of money, or when there is a threat of cruelty or of punishment of loved ones, most people find a way of bending, circumventing, or disregarding truth and institutional loyalties.

More than low breaking points and corruptibility, most people are not very stable. Their judgments are shallow or erratic or both, and the situation is becoming worse. No longer can a contract be secured by a handshake as a pledge and expression of good intent. Now the intent is not so much a desire to carry out the proposition as agreed upon, but rather to see how much the agreement can be evaded under the law.

Going still further, there is the matter of sensitivity. Most people are neither well enough informed nor delicate enough to be aware of needs, conditions, and requirements of others and particularly those who will live a few years hence. In many ways throughout this treatise, attention has been called to ignorance and naiveté as the basis for many kinds of management and governance difficulties. Everybody has ideas about Viet Nam, pollution, and sex education, but how many know the elements of national security, economy, and mental stability involved? To a very great degree, human beings are reckless and irresponsible—and, many have become so calloused they neither care nor sense the totality or the real meaning of problems. Bestial characteristics are just beneath the surface in any society. Release the societal restraints or let the stress build and they break out, sometimes with terrible violence; and let the stress become great enough and even the most staid, the most educated, the most religious, the most devoted, and the most powerful of human beings will resort to violence and jungle behavior.

Man at best is a paradox of extremes. On the one hand, he is humble, understanding, sympathetic, forgiving, and kindly as an angel, and on the other he is an insensitive, self-centered, arrogant, cheating, conniving, and fiendish son-of-a-bitch. A combination of positive and negative tendencies, we submit, is characteristic of all men, high and low, powerful and weak. It is but a matter of how much beneath the surface one must penetrate to reveal humility and compassion in the hardest of personalities, and fracture points with evil and violence in the most staid of individuals. It is with such conflicting qualities that human beings pursue opportunistically the task of advancing civilization—of directing earth cosmology in a manner favorable to human life.

MAN'S OPPORTUNITY TO DIRECT CHANGE

Earlier we arrived directly or indirectly at five general conclusions: (1) that the human species is in an extremely precarious and vulnerable position in Nature's system; (2) that major changes are in the making, inexorably; (3) that the human species pretty much unwittingly is exerting a strong influence on the direction of change; (4) that increasingly, influence of a positive type will be required if the human species is to have a continuing place in Nature's on-going scheme; and (5) that man as a species is neither innately, temperamentally, intellectually, nor experientially well suited for the task of directed global ecology. We now come to a sixth conclusion—that man's central position of control in Nature's scheme is deteriorating badly, and that in the expanding cosmology, man is already being bypassed.

MAN'S DETERIORATING CONTROL

Not only is man possessed with conflicting motives, his naturally emergent value systems have led in directions that now are being disruptively challenged. During the past two decades, some amazing developments have occurred—developments that are profoundly affecting man's position in Nature's scheme. Bullish pioneer confidence, which existed through World War II, has somehow given way to growing disillusionment—so much so, in fact, that there is deteriorating belief in the human purpose as generally defined.

The situation is illustrated poignantly by a statement made recently by a young man with long hair when he said "Dad, I want no part of what your generation has stood for." Of importance here is why such a disturbing and offensive remark was made in the first place, and after that why it has been made in our time. Let us consider the respective vantage points and attempt to view the world through the eyes of both father and son.

The father in all probability went to a one- or two-room grade school where he had a daily regimen of prayer, pledge of allegiance, sportsmanship, and citizenship, fostering attitudes of patriotism, group superiority, and the view that God is naturally on our side. In his development, his idealism and his ideas of virtue became based on the precepts of mother, home, and heaven, and his goal as it emerged was to become an all-American boy with *red blooded guts* flowing in his veins.

The son, in contrast, is a member of the first generation to be influenced strongly by television. During his most impressionable years he has seen life as it is. He has seen people as people wherever they live or whatever their color—that they have pretty much the same problems and pretty much the same aspirations. He sees, too, that they become enemies when boundary lines— sociological or geographical—are drawn to separate them and when their presumed rights are encroached upon.

At the international level, the father, because of earlier indoctrination, sees the nation as the supreme entity and, also because of his indoctrination, he is intellectually and emotionally committed to defend it with his life. He can muster little faith in the United Nations or that for which it stands. In his mind he generates national enemies and he thinks little of human unity. He sees war as the means of reaching clear decisions and of giving substance to nations of people. He sees wars as winnable—with unconditional surrender possibilities, with finalized treaties, and with "rightfully" earned properties or territories. He makes a distinction between the killing of civilians and the killing of people in uniform, even though they may be from the same family and in the same house; the first he sees as murder and the second as a duty—that is, except when the method of killing is all-out bombing when the duty is to kill indiscriminately. He feels that prisoners who were killer bombers only moments before should not only be treated humanely but should be afforded privileges. He feels that the killing of warfare should be done according to rules—the Geneva Conventions. He knows people who participated in World War I and he participated himself in World War II. He knows. He was there. To refuse to participate or even to lack enthusiasm about participating, to him, smacks of treason.

The son, on the other hand, with his generalized knowledge of human behavior, sees the world as a neighborhood, and he sees that the problems of food, living room, health, education, and employment are much the same everywhere irrespective of loyalty, patriotism, political power blocks, or commitments to economic principles. He has older friends who were in the Korean War and he has himself been in Viet Nam. Continuously during his life he has felt the threat of nuclear decimation for whole nations of people. He does not see war as winnable, but rather as stalemates with balanced terror as a kind of holding action. In his comparatively short life, the younger man has seen untold poverty and at the same time the denudation of plains and mountain sides; he has also seen unbelievable wastage of resources in warfare that would help so very much if used positively in the country his military efforts attempted to "secure." He has seen women and children wantonly slaughtered and entire villages burned—all of this causing him to wonder what humanity, democracy and Christianity really mean.

At the national level, the father sees the right of franchise as one of man's most precious privileges inasmuch as it was the reward for a vast and courageous struggle by his forefathers to escape from tyranny. The son instead sees the tyranny of corrupt power politics with a design that perpetuates a widening gap between "in-and-have" groups on the one hand, and "out-and-have-not" groups on the other. The father sees law and order as the answer to protest and rebellion necessitated by public responsibility, whereas the son sees it as repression designed to maintain the status quo with all its evils and shortcomings.

At the personal level, the father sees himself as a paragon of virtue standing for what is right and fair *under the law*. The son sees him as hypocritical, hiding behind *laws that are man-made* and often designed to protect and give sanction for advantages to special interests. The son went on to say "Dad, I have had a belly full. First I will stand against the philosophy and ideology of your generation and then I will formulate my own."

Television undoubtedly has made a significant contribution to the reevaluation that is going on irrespective of generations. Its appearance has coincided fairly closely with the beginning of the Era of Concentration. Growing loss of confidence constitutes growing loss of control in man's societal management role.

Consider also a different type of example—one illustrative of many kinds of deteriorating control. In 1897, under the strong influence of Gifford Pinchot, the United States Forest Service was established in the Department of Agriculture to maintain orderly and integrated management of forested lands. The work included attention to timber, mining, water conservation, and recreation. In 1905 President Theodore Roosevelt declared that the object of forestry was not to "lock up" forests, but "to consider how best to combine use with preservation." In 1924, resulting from the leadership of Aldo Leopold, then Secretary of

Agriculture, a beginning was made in setting aside wilderness areas—that is, areas to be kept unsullied by the hand of man and maintained through the years for observation, enjoyment, and study.

Of significance here is the fact that national forests and wilderness areas have been established and are maintained by democratic action—by majority vote under the influence of differing interest factions. On the one hand there are the ecologic enthusiasts concerned with the maintenance of at least some areas in a pristine state for aesthetic, scientific, and rehabilitative purposes, and on the other hand there are those who make a living from the land by taking the timber, the minerals, and the water, and by building saw mills, gas stations, entertainment centers, and the like. The Forest Service, as designated custodian, is in between with the assigned responsibility of combining use and preservation in the case of national forests and fostering preservation in case of wilderness areas. Both the ecologists and the promoters struggle for rights and privileges, but rights and privileges that are 180 degrees apart with respect to conservation. Again it is a matter of whose rights and privileges get the green light. It is also a matter of whether really satisfactory answers— that is, answers compatible with Nature's requirements—can be obtained by majority vote under the influence of pressure politics. When the forest and wilderness areas were first set aside, the needs for land and job opportunities were not as great as at present, so that there was little opposition to the idea of natural preserves, and there was little difficulty in establishing such. Now, and as time goes along, the needs for jobs and work opportunities are becoming greater, and little by little—by democratic action to be sure—encroachments are made on the preserves, thus endangering the concept of preserves and conservation and risking the loss of natural areas altogether.

The democratic process obviously is not rigid enough to assure indefinite maintenance of natural areas. Under it, the pressures of population will inevitably cause the lifeline to be thrown or the light to be switched in favor of survival at the moment rather than in favor of beauty, pleasure, or longer range scientific interests. The same kind of problem exists in connection with the protection and maintenance of Indian reservations, with protection of the rights and privileges of primitive and under-privileged peoples, with the protection of wildlife, with the conservation of water, and the like. With growing populations, with increasing pollution, and with worsening complexity, the democratic process will be under test and challenge increasingly.

BEYONDNESS

In Nature's grand cavalcade of change, man's central role of societal management and directed destiny can be evaluated in still another way—one that shows man being bypassed in some degree already in the overall development.

For the purposes here, it is important to have in mind four points made earlier: (1) that management of large and complex systems depends on communication and control, (2) that information is the commodity of information and control operation, (3) that information interacting with information is generative, and (4) that self-organizing systems—living or nonliving—generate their own goals and set their own course of action. It is important to have in mind also the process of institutionalization with all of its fortuitous ramifications.

Illustration 1

We see men in high places—businesses, corporations, governments—struggling desperately not only to manage, but more particularly to know what is going on. The problem, as noted earlier, is not so much that of availability of information, but more that of comprehending the great mass of materials that are available. Institutional leaders, of course, take the votes of trustees, of boards of directors, and of stockholders, but the empires over which they have dominion are so vast, and so far-reaching in their influence that neither the leaders nor the people they lead can have confidence that the questions they vote on or the votes taken are really relevant or meaningful.

What is happening increasingly as organizations grow larger and more complex is the use of detectors at way stations throughout the organizations or systems that sense trends and give a signal when a particular condition is reached. In a large mercantile system, for example, when an inventory drops below a certain level, reorder is activated by the system itself. Similarly, when earnings have reached a certain point, dividends are kicked out

automatically. It is true that many such functions are yet performed by human beings, but they do not need to be—not even
the functions of deciding whether a particular process or business
is failing and should discontinue, or whether a change of policy
is needed. All that a human being does in the decision-making
process of larger organizations is weigh the evidence pro and con
with respect to particular questions and make a judgment based
on limitations and certain principles and goals as decided on.
All of these kinds of functions, including goal definition and redefinition, can now be done by machines, often with more satisfaction since any biases must be willfully programmed in and
and thereby made fully apparent.

As detecting, decision-making, and goal-determination devices
are located as needed at strategic points in large and complex
systems, the systems themselves take on a character and behavior
and become amazingly efficient in performing the whole operational role more or less on their own. Man's part, therefore, not
only becomes less but also less significant.

Illustration 2

An outstanding example of "beyondness" is operation of the
United States military establishment. It is ubiquitous. It extends everywhere, both inside and outside the country. Its far-
reaching and powerful influence is beyond the comprehension and
understanding of the people who support it with their labors and
their taxes. In many ways, it is beyond the comprehension and
understanding of the Joint Chiefs of Staff and of the Commander-
in-Chief even with the vast in-flow of information. If, then, we
add the undercover work of intelligence organizations, the action
and influence becomes still more unfathomable. Justification for
the activities, of course, is defense, but the influence goes much
further—and in ways that are almost incomprehensible. Employment both at home and abroad is markedly augmented. Econ-
omies are reshaped and in some instances caused to disappear.
Educational policies are augmented and redirected. Human integrity is manipulated like a pawn. Morality is set on a different
course. Even the genetic pattern is hybridized and populations
bastardized in some degree. The United States military is a large
and complex organization. It lives and breathes and it has a behavior of its own. It functions by means of people, but it is in a way

above and beyond people. Even the United States Congress, which provides support, is powerless to know in significant detail about its action or to do more than increase or decrease the financing a little. The United States military, as mentioned earlier, is a juggernaut loose on the world and it is almost impossible for human society to do anything about it.

Illustration 3

Governments are also large and complex systems. They are far-reaching and it is impossible for administrators to be aware of the influence of their expansive agencies. Again the problem is not so much a lack of information as it is an ability to comprehend the meaning of that which is available. As in the case of businesses and corporations, votes are taken and decisions are made, but with agonizing question regarding relevancy. Also, as in the case of other complex organizations, the leadership action is becoming less consequential. Leaders may be replaced, agencies may come and go, administrations may change, and revolutions may even occur, but societal management goes on and with features that are basically the same irrespective of policies or leadership. The population must have food, there must be reasonable freedom from disease, and there must be aspirations. A society will provide these things for itself by the simple process of surviving. Anything beyond represents a kind of nonvital trimming. Strength in *large* systems lies more in the systems themselves than in the leadership at any given time or in the people they presume to serve.

Illustration 4

The point becomes even more strongly emphasized when considered in connection with the NASA Moon Shot Program. Here communication and control have been enormously complex with many locations on the earth and in space being linked together. Much information was stored in computers to be drawn upon as needed—much more in fact than could be stored in a single or even a group of minds. Man and machines were on line together, both men and machines were making decisions as questions arose. Once the goals were set—man, moon, decade—the program played through like a record, making adjustments and overcoming hazards and failures along the way. As the system developed, man's role became less and less significant. Men could drop out and subsystems could fail, but the overall program could go on.

Illustration 5

Our point becomes still more strongly emphasized by remembering from information dynamics that information interacting with information is generative, and that we are now in the midst of an information explosion. There is a tendency on the part of human beings to attribute the amazing newer scientific and technical developments to man's increasing intelligence. The facts are that the information system itself governs these developments to a very large degree. One discovery opens the way for development of the next. One discovery lays an information foundation for the development of new information, and new information has a way of being pervasive. Important discoveries, as they come, often are made by several people in different places at essentially the same time, simply because the time was right. It is fully apparent that if Roentgen had not discovered X rays when he did, or that if Madam Curie had not discovered radium when she did, the same discoveries would have been made by any one of a number of other people, and probably during the coming year. Information is an increasingly significant element in Nature's system of earth cosmology, and man appears as a kind of innocent pawn tuned to respond to information stimuli as they appear. In Nature's operation, man has been a means by which information is developed, but increasingly the information systems created by man are taking over and in certain respects, ruling him.

The illustrations emphasize the idea that whereas man, on the one hand, is performing ever more brilliantly in the design and development of systems, on the other he is becoming less significant in directing his own destiny as ever larger and more complex systems come to perform their functions. An important question is what man's position will be as still larger systems, including the vast stores of information in our libraries, are interconnected and their functions integrated.

Man's individual, and even his collective, leadership role in the period ahead is in considerable doubt. Large systems, organizations, and institutions, with their self-organizing and self-perpetuating capabilities tend to survive and exert their influence despite the human beings involved in the operation. Very often, individuals and substantial groups of individuals disappear without making a significant difference. Increasingly, it appears that about the only way to eliminate large institutions is to starve them to death—to cut off their source of sustenance and let them die. However, when the system or institution is a monopoly or a sovereign power, even this approach is difficult or untenable. Such considerations cause us to have even stronger impressions of the concept of beyondness.

CIVILIZATION'S TENUOUS COURSE

In light of the earth's ecosystem limitations, it has been easy enough to look at man's behavior, to find weak spots in his conduct with respect to long-range species survival, and to point out probable disaster if certain practices are continued. It has also been easy to visualize a more ideal or utopian situation that would be expected to result if man were to dispose of his primitive opportunistic seat-of-the-pants techniques and resort to more carefully reasoned and determined approaches to problem resolution. What direction, then, is man likely to go, the situation, the tendencies, and the trends being what they are?

On the basis of points made throughout this text, let us list somewhat in the order of priority, key changes that man obviously must make as requirements for continued societal existence. They are:

1. Stabilization of population.
2. Elimination of warfare.
3. Replacement of the concept of nationalism with that of human unity.
4. Making employment and earning a living of the whole people dependent on other than inflation and armaments.
5. Reliance more on positive moment-to-moment problem resolutions than on fixed laws and regulations.
6. Emphasis on quality of life, including mutual trust and respect, rather than wealth and power.

Realization of such objectives would probably be classed by

any analyst as utopian. If they, or features closely related, are requirements for continuing societal survival, what then is societal man likely to do as he faces the future?

Because societal man is opportunistic and reacts to emergencies more than to needs irrespective of how apparent, because he tends to deal with symptoms more than with causes, because he tends to deal with small pieces of societal problems more than with whole problems, and because action people rarely look ahead further than the next election, it is predicted that societal groups will do very little—that is, unless there is somehow a profound awakening, such as a collapse of atmospheric sustaining power in noteworthy industrial communities, of widespread famine, or of World War III.

That the world ecosystem requires management like a *balanced aquarium* is becoming more evident to all thoughtful people. It is clear to the young man who said "Dad, I want no part of what your generation has stood for." It is clear to the serious-minded activist who talks openly and frankly about human ecology. It is clearer to minority than to majority groups, and it is clearer to "out-and-have-not" groups than to the "in-and-have." Demonstrations and insurrections, although deplorable, are causing more people to sense and to be more keenly aware of global ecology as a phenomenology to be dealt with in our time. But will concern become profound soon enough?

Chapter 12

Cybernation: An Approach to the Future

We have concluded that human civilization is on course with its own demise, and that degradative changes are underway leading to disaster in the not-too-distant future unless strong societal action is taken quite soon. A conclusion also reached was that human society, left to its usual responsiveness and behavior, is not likely to take preventive steps that will have more than a delaying action.

These conclusions constitute a shocking and intensely disturbing judgment. They are fatalistic in extreme.

There are, of course, many positive aspects of human life, especially in the fields of science and technology, to which attention could have been directed, but the objective has been to detect soft spots and fracture points in societal behavior, doing so at a time when social problems of great magnitude are being intensified.

We have said that major changes will probably occur in the fairly near future, and it is important to have firmly in mind the reasons why. They are based, it will be remembered, on ideas as follows. If population growth continues at present rates, there would be one person for each square foot of land area on the face of the earth in about 600 years with suffocating stagnation due to occur much sooner—possibly a century or even less. Such, without equivocation, would be a major change. On the other hand, if population is somehow slowed sufficiently to avoid or to postpone the stagnation and strangulation, this also would constitute a major change. Stabilization of population would mean yielding on the pioneer-chamber-of-commerce ideas of growth; it would mean a necessary shift from wealth distribution based on expanding employment to one based on more fixed employment; and it would mean digression from the philosophy of accommodating all the human beings that sexual passion might generate. Because of what will happen on the basis of population behavior alone, we say there will be major changes in the comparatively near future; but, we call attention also to the more profound and subtle threatening determiners that would, if not controlled, hasten or precipitate the degradation: namely, the widening separation between "haves" and "have-nots," the growing gap between educated and noneducated, runaway inflation, armaments strangulation, and nuclear war—among others.

Two questions remain: Is there a way to avert, offset, or replace the seemingly inevitable degradative trend? What would be required as a minimum to restore generalized respect for and confidence in the human cause as part of Nature's grand scheme?

ADAPTIVE POTENTIATION

In Chapter 11, a list of requirements for continued societal existence was set forth. Included was elimination of warfare, deemphasis on nationalism, and emphasis on human unity, making employment and earning a living dependent on constructive occupations instead of armaments and inflation, reliance more on rational societal behavior than on fixed laws and regulations, and emphasis on quality of life. With the basic instincts, drives, precepts, and needs of the human species being what they are, there is little reason to expect that human society will of its own volition give serious attention to such matters in time to offset effectively the degradative processes now in the making. Strangely, however, there are reasons for expecting that the listed requirements, impossible as they may seem, will be realized to some extent automatically irrespective of deliberate human efforts to achieve social improvement.

Attention has been called to the fact that complex communication and control systems are transcending man to assume data gathering, and analytical and management functions, thus leaving man as a kind of necessary design unit in the overall system. Such systems transcend man in management functions also because they are less irascible, are free of human traditions, biases and self-interests, and therefore are more rational and more dependable. World cybernation, linking together large data banks and programmed to detect and automatically initiate and direct the action required to avert critical trends, it is suggested, not only could but will be a means of overcoming at least some of man's most serious predicaments.

First, with world communication and control opportunities being what they are, there is the prospect that global ecosystem management of production, conservation, and utilization of world resources could be achieved. Second, with world ecosystem management as a natural and reasonable development, the features of intense nationalism, warfare, armaments, and inflation would become superfluous, and in time would fade away and disappear. Further, with improving cybernation, states and communities would be able to free themselves of local biases and to manage their own affairs more completely, making it unnecessary to send taxes to the national capital for distribution back to the states and communities (often in diminished amounts and with strings attached), thereby reducing the need for strong centralized governments and for politicians (inevitably committed by the political system) as representatives. With still further improvement in cybernation enabling factions of society and even individuals to be connected directly with the overall communication and control systems with dataphones and by means of actual man-machine linkage, human society would in reality become integrated to function as an advanced societal system (Level 3, Figure 29), and thus be able to avoid much of the discrimination, insecurity, and unrest so characteristic of poorly coordinated societal systems.

We recognize as beyond present approaches to societal problems the idea of cybernation and ecogaming as a means for achieving necessary societal improvements, but we ask whether there can be any other sensible and rational way—human developments being what they have been. We have pointed out that ideological planning and promotion in the usual manner cannot be expected to exert much influence for improvement so that it becomes a matter of importance to examine the systems management approach of cybernetics for the force and impact it may have.

As an outgrowth of man's mentative emergence, the trend toward communication and control by means of networks, data banks, and computers is enormously strong. It is the kind of direction human beings can go, are going, and are likely to continue to go in the near future. It is the direction they will go if the mentative function continues to evolve. The practical trends, even if not the ideological, are by their inherent nature toward a kind of human unity. We ask whether nationalistic chauvinism is likely to stand for long in the face of such world developments, whether a system of fixed and poorly adapted laws can stand in the face of societal behavior closely coordinated by cybernetic processes, and whether the gaps between "haves" and "have-nots" and between educated and noneducated can stand for long in the face of increasingly better-informed peoples. We offer the view that human society should not only expect and prepare itself for rapid trends in cybernation, but that it should foster and encourage them as a practical means of achieving vital societal improvements.

DIRECTED POTENTIATION

In the section just preceding, no mention was made of one of the requirements for continued societal existence listed in Chapter 11 —stabilization of population. Although cybernation could and would provide an accurate indication of societal procreative needs in accordance with some selected policy, it would not exert an automatic regulating influence on the reproductive process in the same way that it would in the case of various other aspects of human function—certainly not within confines of the reproductive process as it now operates.

Reproduction, at least at present, is strictly a human prerogative, and not one that can be augmented very much by outside influences—machine or otherwise. Earlier we indicated that man by his reproductive action will, to a very large degree, determine whether the human species will continue on a degradative course of increasing congestion and deterioration, or have the opportunity to turn toward a more assured positive way of life. Now we can emphasize that man, by his reproductive action, will largely determine whether the human species will continue on a degradative course or create the opportunity for worldwide cybernation and global ecosystem management, thereby opening a new frontier compatible with the situation in which the human species now finds itself. It is now fully evident that man's societal decision and action with respect to reproduction in the next few decades will go a long way toward determining whether human civilization will have a future.

Reproduction combines with child rearing and education in the creation of operative human beings. Human society is not only producing new individuals at an unprecedented and threatening rate, it is indoctrinating and surrounding them with precedents and customs in such a way as to preclude attention to the question of numbers and thereby interfere with giving attention to the quality of people. Population is a problem that would be overcome by steps as simple and as sensible as asking and requiring parents to have no more than two or three children —a situation now attainable with existing contraceptive procedures and with legalized abortion available as means for correcting mistakes. Such action would represent little in the way of denial at the family level, and most families, in accord with their own wishes and conclusions, would be better off from many points of view. Actually, resistance is not so much at the family level as it is at the economic, political, and religious levels. Children maturing into adults are needed to maintain the markets, to insure voting strength, and to provide souls for the kingdom of heaven—the assumption in all three cases being: "the more the better."

Not only has man functioned poorly in developing views about desirable numbers of human beings, he has done badly also in rearing and training, often producing offspring that are insecure and lack confidence in the society of which they are a part. As population pressures grow stronger and degradation becomes more intense—as seems inevitable even if strong control measures are not initiated very soon—question may well arise whether reproduction, rearing, and training may not be regarded as too important to be left to chance genetics, to sexual passions, to hit-or-miss rearing by career parents, and to strongly biased teaching; indeed, the question may be whether they are not too precious to be left to teachers and parents in their respective roles. Genetic improvement and artificial insemination techniques are already well perfected and in use; artificial ovination and artificial gestation are now only matters of technology; and group rearing is already well tested. When societal man is willing to yield on a few matters like pioneer growth, inheritance laws, pride of parenthood, and the necessity of parental love, and there is a will to do so, management of population will not be difficult. This step is a matter of decision, one to be made in people's minds and not by external cybernetic processes. Moreover, it is a decision that will be made by giving careful attention or by inadvertent or willful neglect.

REQUIREMENTS FOR RENEWED RESPECT AND CONFIDENCE

We have talked about the young man who wanted no part of what his father's generation stood for, we have made reference to insurrection on the part of minority "out-and-have-not" groups, we have discussed what can be called *"big-daddyism"* on the part of "in-and-have" groups, and we have considered at length the generalized unrest existent among different factions of people. To the extent possible, it is important to indicate the conditions required to restore some semblance of mutual respect and confidence about the future. Such an undertaking is hazardous, but we can begin by considering what would be required to produce mutual respect between the young man and his father—and, for purposes of convenience, we shall refer to this young man as Jonathan-X.

When one sits with college students who are wearing the symbols of contempt—as does Jonathan-X on occasion—and whose questions reveal decline or complete loss of respect for and confidence in "the establishment," meaning the whole societal system, including government, academia, and many kinds of personal relationships, some idea of inner feelings can be obtained by taking note of the kinds of speakers and ideas that draw applause and bring forth standing ovations. It is my impression that such speakers are those that are convincingly honest, completely candid, and willing to cut into hypocrisy wherever it exists. It is my impression also that noncollege assemblies of the present period respond in the same way, although more with resignation than with the student reaction of determination to see a change.

With speakers coming mainly from political, governmental, economic, and academic institutions, students and others find few to whom they will render a standing ovation or even give courteous attention. Hypocrisy, deceptiveness, and dishonesty, as we are so painfully aware, are widespread and pervasive in essentially all establishment organizational entities. When, then, a stalemate on morality combines with a stalemate on population management, as is happening, the problem of restoring faith and confidence of young Jonathan-X, his father, and their contemporaries, becomes even more difficult.

The arrogance and the advantage of "in-and-have" groups is difficult to break. In democratic countries, they have the majority vote and the power, and there is no inclination to yield or share it. Being in good earning positions, they see social problems in terms of law and order and a little charity or social welfare. The situation in our period, however, is becoming much more stressful inasmuch as "out-and-have-not" groups are becoming proportionately larger and thus are exerting an ever-increasing influence. For them existing laws, employment practices, and wealth distribution procedures (wages, savings, and investment) act to keep them in a depressed status; for them existing laws in many cases are a hindrance and therefore to be disobeyed without getting caught or to be discredited altogether. Common misery unites the minorities, the unemployed, the disgruntled, and the disillusioned and modern communication unites them with some effectiveness throughout the world—which, as has been pointed out, is making for a new kind of world unity. Because of widespread knowledge of modern weaponry and because of the extreme vulnerability of large and interdependent modern cities, gorilla warfare and the induction of terror into "in-and-have" groups is quite easy—so easy, in fact, that anonymous threats often have a widespread disruptive influence. Even simple nonviolent demonstrations challenging the policies and moral principles of institutions have been found sufficient to topple leaderships or even to bring down institutions not well founded in the general public interest. The response of "in-and-have" groups, instead of correcting for revealed weaknesses, is often to endure the status quo and to insist on stronger repressive action, steps that intensify the discontent and contribute to an expanding underground movement. Confidence in the future for either Jonathan-X or his father and others is difficult to restore when there are growing signs of worldwide civil war and when the leaders of "in-and-have" groups lack the sensitivity to see, the ability to interpret the trends, or the intelligence to recognize and deal with underlying causes.

This less-than-inspiring picture provides backdrop for still another matter of concern to young Jonathan-X and his confreres. Suppose that somehow human society would resolve its problems of population, morality, and unity, thus moving into a kind of utopian situation. There then would be the question of how much tranquility the human species could stand. Life arose and evolution has occurred in face of continuing hardship—probably because of it in some measure. We have agreed with Ardrey in saying that after the body is sustained in health with food and living room, there are two basic requirements for human life: identity and stimulus. Hardship, including warfare, has given opportunity for identity, and it has provided the most significant opportunities for stimulus. Utopia would have boredom as a major hazard unless stimulus is provided by other means.

To satisfy Jonathan-X, his father, and other thoughtful people of the present period, and cause them to have a renewed faith in mankind and a feeling of optimism about the future, we restate and extend the requirements for societal survival, listing the following as a minimum:

1. A realistic facing of the population problem together with steps to maintain a growing economy without growth in numbers of people.

2. A realistic move toward global ecology designed to foster preservation, conservation, and fair and equitable use of natural resources.

3. A realistic move toward human unity, including recognition of the world as a neighborhood and of the human population as a single species to be treated justly and fairly throughout.

4. A realistic effort to deemphasize nationalism and to eliminate war.

5. A realistic effort to erase the gaps between the "in-and-have" and the "out-and-have-not" groups and between the educated and noneducated.

6. A realistic move against hypocrisy in business, government, education, and other aspects of human life.

7. A realistic move to maintain the economy—especially employment—by means other than armaments and inflation.

Point (8) then would be provision of satisfying stimulus by means other than warfare and competitive exploitation.

The price for optimism about the future thus is very high—but more in terms of human attitudes, it would seem, than of money and effort. With respect to a number of fundamental, cherished, and long-standing concepts of human life and behavior, complete shifts in philosophy would be required—and, among other things, the questions of tyranny versus democracy, and of honesty versus perversion and deception will of necessity have to be reconsidered and acted on all over again. These are not easy steps for human society to take, but it is no longer a question of ease or feasibility; it is one of whether action will be taken to reach for the remaining lifeline. Confidence in the future with lessening tensions can be expected only when there is evidence of this kind of action.

SOCIAL LIBERATION

Revolutions of the past have been particularistic, supported mainly by minority groups seeking to assert their own specific interests over those of society as a whole. The great middle-class revolutions of modern times have offered ideologies of sweeping political reconstitution, but in reality did little more than to certify the social dominance of middle-class groups and to give formal expression to the economic ascendancy of industrial capitalism. The lofty notions of "nation," "free citizen," and "equality" conceal the reality of the centralized state and the dominance of bourgeois aspirations.

By creating vast urban agglomerations of concrete, metal, and glass, by overriding and undermining the complex and subtly organized ecosystems that constitute local differences in the natural world—in short, be replacing the highly complex organic process by a simplified inorganic one—the prevailing society is disassembling the biotic pyramid that has supported humanity for millenia. Moreover, in the course of replacing the complex ecologic relationships, this society is restoring the biosphere to a stage that will support only simpler forms of life. This is seen most clearly in the sweeping urban belts of America and Europe where synthetic materials tend to replace every living feature of the natural environment.

The same processes of simplification occur in the countryside, where mass production of food transforms the traditional farmstead into an agricultural factory based on monoculture, chemical controls, and insensate large-scale mechanization—often with savage disregard of the vitalizing natural ecology.

But these changes are not limited to the biological realm alone. They are carried directly to every facet of human life. In the great cities, swollen to the bursting point by quantities of people, only a mass concept of life can prevail. The need to employ, to feed, to educate, to protect, and to transport millions of human beings daily, reinforces the centralistic, totalitarian, and bureaucratic tendencies that subsist under modern industrial capitalism. If it achieved nothing else, middle-class society revolutionized the means of resources utilization and the manufacture of products on a scale unprecedented in history. The resulting bureaucratic scale, reared on urban gigantism and the logistics of mass control, replaces the human scale. Life becomes faceless and as homogenized as the manipulative apparatus itself. The wealth of social experience that marked earlier periods of history falls away, revealing man as an object, as a mass manufactured commodity— the product of social factories euphemistically called the "family," the "school," the "home," the "church," and the "community."

The reactive responses of rebellious youth have produced invaluable forms of libertarian and utopian affirmation—the right to make love without restriction, the goal of community in group living, disavowal of monetary and commodity worth as such, belief in mutual assistance, and a new respect for spontaneity and individuality. Easy as it is for persons of experience and tradition to point out the pitfalls of recent youthful behavior, it has played a preparatory role of decisive importance in forming the atmosphere of indiscipline, individuality, balance, and freedom.

What is unique about our own period is that the particularistic revolution is being transcended by a generalized revolution brought about by social forces and the inexorable processes of nature. The technological revolution leading into cybernation and adaptive societal behavior is creating opportunity for a world without class dominance, dangerous exploitation, drudgery, ill health, and material want—that is, assuming inundation and obliteration by swarming populations can be avoided. Means are now available for development of the rounded man—for development of the total man, free of guilt, free of authoritarian modes of indoctrination, and free of the sensuous compulsion for bigness and growth. This is the situation, not only because Nature is demanding it, but also because it is possible at the present state of enlightenment to conceive of a future experience in terms of a coherent process—one in which the bifurcation of thought and activity, of mind and consciousness, of discipline and spontaneity, of individuality and community, of man and nature, of town and country, of education and life, of work and play—all are resolved, harmonized, and organically united qualitatively in an updated concept of freedom. Just as the particularized revolution produced a particularized bifurcated society, the generalized revolution now emerging could be expected to produce an organically unified and many-sided type of community and species life. The great wound opened by emergent propertied society could and can be healed.

Freedom for the future, if it is to have realistic rationality with respect to human social goals, must be conceived in human more than in materialistic goals—in terms of life and not mere survival. Men do not remove their ties of bondage and become completely human merely by divesting themselves of social domination, or by obtaining freedom in abstract form. They must also be free in mind and spirit in such a way that the working of the mentative information process can achieve its action and provide its transconstitutive rewards. They must become even more human as mentative creatures.

The question continues to be whether there is a redemptive process that will transform human social development from its present negativistic trends into positive action in such a way that individual human beings will in reality attain control over their daily lives, or whether we must accept that human advancement must end with industrial capitalism.

The absolute negation of city is *community*—a situation where the social environment is decentralized into rounded ecologically balanced biomes. The absolute negation of bureaucracy is *immediate and direct interaction*—a situation where representation is replaced by immediate adaptiveness. The absolute negation of centralized economy is *regional biotechnology*—a situation where the instruments of production are molded with the productive potential of the ecological community.

It is not accidental that at a point in history when hierarchical power and manipulation have reached the points of greatest influence, that the very concepts of hierarchy, power, and manipulation are being effectively challenged by probing questions, cutting demonstrations, and insurrection. Challenge to these concepts comes from discovery of the importance of spontaneity and unrestrained interaction, especially in the information generative process—a discovery nourished by ecology, by a heightened concept of self-development, and by a new understanding of the adaptive process inherent in the cybernetic features of societal operation.

What ecology is showing is that balance is achieved by organic differentiation and complexity, not by homogeneity and simplification. The more varied the flora and fauna of a biome, the more stable are the populations of the system. The more environmental diversity is diminished, the more the population support potential for a particular species fluctuates with the greater probability that its survival will be threatened. Left to itself, a biome tends spontaneously toward organic differentiation, greater flora and fauna, and diversity in number of prey and predators. This does not mean, however, that interference by man for his own benefits must necessarily be avoided in order to keep the system vigorous and productive.

The need for a productive agriculture—itself a form of interference with nature—must always remain in the foreground of an ecological approach to food cultivation and forest management. No less important is the fact than man can often produce changes in the biome that vastly improve its ecologic and thereby its productive quality. Such efforts, however, necessitate insight and understanding and not the exercise of excessive force and ruthless environmental augmentation. Survival and advancement of the human species in the future will not be by randomized, hit-and-miss, seat-of-the-pants techniques, but by intelligent planning and design—by managed ecology. It will be by intelligent and effective ecogamesmanship.

This concept of management, this new regard for spontaneity and adaptiveness, has far-reaching implications for technology and commuunity—indeed for the very image of man in civilized society. It challenges the capitalistic ideal of agriculture as a factory operation organized around immense centrally controlled land holdings, highly specialized forms of monoculture, the reduction of the terrain to the factory floor, the substitution of organic by chemical processes, the use of brute power and gang labor, and the like. If food cultivation is to be more in accordance with planned ecology than with the contest of opponents, the agriculturists must of necessity be familiar with capability of the land and be able to potentiate functions meaningfully and efficiently. They must acquire a new sensitivity to its needs and its use for dependent societies. This presupposes an elevation of agriculture to a human rather than an economic scale and the restoration of moderate-sized agricultural units—in short, a decentralized and ecologically balanced system of food production used for the support of reasonable populations, a simplistic rather than complex societal organization.

The same reasoning applies to industry in connection with the manufacture of products and pollution control. The development of giant factory complexes in regional localities, drawing resource materials from all parts of the world, and the use of single and dual energy sources to the exclusion of others, creates risks of major technological failures and at the same time invites attack by insurrectionists. Only by developing smaller industrial units utilizing clean power sources, such as solar radiation, wind power, and water power in balance with the number of users, will it be possible to reduce significantly the scourge of industrial pollution, eliminate the harassment of overcomplexity, prevent the catastrophies of large power outages, stop the devastation caused by strikes, remove the tyranny of big government, avoid the boredom of uniformity, and achieve the identification, stimulus, and security necessary for civilized living.

The implications of smaller scale diversified and decentralized community agriculture, industry, and government are obvious. If man is to use the cybernetic principles needed or required for ecosystem management, both society and the basic units of society must operate as integrated ecosystems—as systems with purpose and goals and with adaptive management potential. They, too, must become diversified and well-rounded, thus avoiding the widening gaps between "haves" and "have-nots." This concept of community life is anchored in the utopian ideal of the rounded man—the individual whose sensitivities, range of experience, and life style are nourished by a wide range of stimuli, by a diversity of activities, by the generativeness of an active intellect, by the adaptiveness and increasing options of highly developed communication and control, and by a social scale that remains continuously within the comprehension and reach of the single human being. The means and conditions of survival become the means and conditions for life; need becomes desire and desire becomes need. The condition is achieved in which the greatest social decomposition provides the source of a higher form of social integration, bringing the most pressing ecological necessities into common focus with high utopian ideals.[1]

SUMMARY POINTS

A strong feature of this treatise has been recognition of an inexorable envelopment—one inherent in what human society has tended to regard as natural trends. Its central message is that the human species, with a most impressive record of advancement utilizing primitive and pioneer methods combined with advanced mentative procedures, has arrived at a point in the overall cosmic scheme where continued advancement will require major shifts in attitudes and conduct with respect to reproduction, economic growth, energy development, industrialization, employment, the environment and conflict resolution—to mention only some. Strong emphasis has been placed on the idea that unless substantial progress in transition is made, the human species faces the likelihood of being thrown into a period of decline that would make the former Dark Ages seem like the light of day by comparison. The transition, as indicated, would more than anything else mean further elaboration of man's own area of specialization —that of mentative potentiation.

FINAL COMMENTS

This is a disturbing book. It is a call for action in the field of human ecology—action more urgent than appreciated by the Author as a beginning was made to develop an orderly pattern of thought about man's emergence, his progression, and where he seems to be going. The information set forth constitutes a mandate to those whose business it is to shape and develop attitudes —a mandate to all to somehow make human thought more compatible with reality. In particular, it is a mandate to those in education, in research, in the public media, in government, and in the work of affecting the young during their most impressionable years. The emergent ideas emphasize the need for

[1] In connection with this Section, the writer has borrowed freely from the thoughts and phraseology developed and used by Murray Bookchin for a related but quite different purpose (*Anarchos*, Spring, 1969). Particular indebtedness is hereby expressed.

bringing about the cybernation required to make global eco-system management possible.

The emerging ideas have in no way comprised a mandate to *Save Tomorrow by Opposing Progress* (STOP), but rather to *Save Tomorrow by Advancing Rational Thought* (START). The need again is for a simple faith—a specific and direct philosophy in which people everywhere can have respect and confidence.

In this presentation, much has been said about the oppression of warfare as an instrument of policy, yet nothing has been said implying virtue in reckless abandonment of arms or the neglect of defense. Much has been said about restraints imposed by nationalistic chauvinism, yet nothing has been said against country loyalty. The point repeatedly stressed is that our first loyalty should be to the human species—to human unity—thereby avoiding and preventing the envelopment that increasingly is enshrouding us. Human society is on the verge of great greatness. We ask whether it would not necessarily have to be regarded as a cosmic calamity to miss the opportunity.

Throughout this text, the term *Nature* has been personalized. It has been easier that way. The natural system operates with such precision, with such masterful control, and with such final authority, that it appears to act with personality. Whether life and intellect occurred as an accident on planet earth or were due to emerge inevitably once planet earth was set aside as it was, is impossible to know at the present stage of understanding. The handiwork of the overall determining process is magnificent to observe and inspiring to analyze. We have called it "Nature." Others might choose to call it God.

Index

About the author . . .

Paul S. Henshaw's first book on human ecology and human behavior was published in 1955 and its title was "Adaptive Human Fertility." It, too, dealt with population and the earth's sustaining power. Meanwhile, books have been edited and scientific papers published in the fields of experimental embryology, radiation biology, radiation life shortening, environmental radiation hazards, international public health, information biology and human ecology. Dr. Henshaw was a Co-leader of the first Atomic Bomb Casualty Commission to Japan in 1946; he was Assistant Director of the Division of International Health of the U.S. Public Health Service in the late 1940's; he was Director of Research of the Planned Parenthood Federation of America in the early 1950's and published the first scientific paper on fertility control by physiologic means—i.e. The Pill (*Science*, 1953); he was Project Representative for research funding in the Division of Biology and Medicine of the U.S. Atomic Energy Commission, serving as Editor of Volume 26 on Nuclear Medicine for the United Nations First Geneva Conference on Peaceful Uses of Atomic Energy (1958), and organizer, promoter and editor of the proceedings of the U.S. Atomic Energy Commission Conference on "Radiation Life-shortening: Inventory of Capability" (1963), in the late 1950's and early 1960's; and he was Founding Editor of the journal *Human Potential* in the late 1960's. In most of the activities, there were multiple determiners to consider, and the task in numerous instances was to compare and evaluate opposing risks. The author thus has had extensive experience in the broad field of Human Ecology.

Of related interest . . .

NATURAL SELECTION IN HUMAN POPULATIONS

The Measurement of Ongoing Genetic Evolution in Contemporary Societies

Edited by CARL JAY BAJEMA, Grand Valley State College, and Harvard Center for Population Studies

The 25 papers in this collection of readings measure ongoing human evolution in such contemporary societies as India, Poland, Canada, United States, Russia, Africa, and Japan.

They examine natural selection in relation to physical factors—race, height, weight, headform and congenital defects; disease—malaria, smallpox, cystic fibrosis and degenerative cardiovascular disease; behavior—Tay-Sachs disease, Huntington's Chorea, Schizophrenia and Intelligence; and the future genetic composition of human populations—medical advances, planned parenthood, artificial insemination, the eugenic hypothesis and population control.

The editor supplies an introduction and a selected bibliography for each section.

JOHN WILEY AND SONS, Inc.
605 Third Avenue, New York, N.Y. 10016
New York • London • Sydney • Toronto

ISBN 0-471-3730